FOOD FOR YOUR SOUL

by

Beverley Griffiths

Copyright © 2013

All rights reserved – Beverley Griffiths

No part of this book may be reproduced or transmitted in any form or by any means, graphic, electronic, or mechanical, including photocopying, recording, taping, or by any information storage retrieval system, without the permission, in writing, from the publisher.

Unless otherwise indicated, Bible quotations are taken from the King James Version. Copyright © 1982, Thomas Nelson, Inc., Publishers

Front cover illustration by Steve Williams
Supportive images sourced from Dreamstime.com

Purpose Publishing
United Kingdom
ISBN: 978-0-9570550-2-5

Printed in the United Kingdom

Acknowledgements

First and foremost I would like to thank God for Blessing me with the ability to convey these beautiful words to paper and for giving me the strength and determination to fight Life's battles.

I am truly grateful for God's presence in my life and His love for me is evident each day as I travel the pathways of life. Gods timing is absolutely perfect in all things.

Thank you Lord, I shall stand in great congregations and praise your holy name, for you are truly worthy to be praised. Lord as I walk this path you have laid for me, I ask that you walk with me, because I need you each and every day, every step of the way.

I would like to thank Pastor Sean Samuels, Reverend Everton Lewis Gordon, Reverend Sharon Lewis Gordon, and members of the New Generation Church for all their support and love on my spiritual journey.

I would also like to give special thanks to Minister Barbara Douglas and Sister Dorothy Livingstone who lead the intercessors. Thank you for your support love and prayers.

Special thanks also goes to Sister Maureen Taylor for her time, encouragement, prayers, her continuous support throughout our friendship and for helping me with this vision.

I would like to thank my Mother Loveta who kept me strong with encouragement, care, support and love. She nurtured me and loved me unconditionally.

A Special thank you to my wonderful children   Shantell, Natasha, Aran and Jessica who give me so much love each day.

To Aunty Esther for her kind words of love, her caring ways and her continual request that the Lord bless me! Thanks Aunty for your encouragement and support.

Thank you to my wonderful sister Laverne who's love, encouragement and vision has helped me through difficult times. She spurred me on when impediments came my way. Big thanks Sis!

Thank you to my delightful niece Charlene who helped me in making this book a reality and assisting with compiling the manuscript of this wonderful book.

Special thanks to my true friends, Sharon and Beverley for being who you both are. "Good friends are hard to find but I have found two very good ones"! Thanks for your support and love over the years.

To Pamela my childhood friend who never changed. A true friend who has given me encouragement and has supported me along this journey.

So Lord, I thank you for placing me in such a wonderful family and giving me fantastic true friends.

I am truly blessed.

To God be the glory forevermore.

Tribute to Absent Love Ones

A Tribute to my wonderful father *Derrick*, uncle *Jerry* and my best friend *Sister Vera,* who are sadly no longer with us, but are always in our thoughts. Your memories live on and the love you left remains with us and will never be forgotten.

Love you always...

About the Author

Beverley is a woman who possesses determination and tenacity when fighting life's battles. She has faced many difficult times and situations but her personal relationship with the Lord has helped her to overcome heartbreaking situations along the journey of her life.

She is a woman who believes in elevating and encouraging men and women, the young and elders to reach their potential, to seek the purpose for which the Lord called them to be in the Kingdom.

You can expect one hundred percent commitment in whatever she does; she gives with a willing heart and an abundance of love.

Her writings are truly inspirational and spiritually uplifting. They offer a source of hope and comfort to the reader.

She is A Blessed Woman of God

Sharon Miller- Lewinson

From the Author

In October 2003, 19 days after my father passed away I was grieving heavily. One morning approximately 9:30am I heard the audible voice of the Lord, somehow I knew I had to write down what I heard, I grabbed the nearest thing which was an envelope which previously contained my phone-bill.

I began to write down what I heard and this is what the Lord said to me;

"God time is prefect! It is flawless! It is not mans time, it's God's time."

He does nothing before the time, sometimes we may say, I have prayed for something and not received an answer to my prayer, but He answers us in His time because His time is prefect

Sometimes He leaves us in awesome wonder at His impeccable timing, because everything is done in his time.

He said to my father:

"you have laboured hard my son, you love your family dearly but now you are tired! Close your eyes my son and I will take you home with me for eternal rest, don't worry about your loved ones. I will send the comforter to ease the pain and grief they feel, that they will come to know that you are surely with me and at peace!"

These words brought me great comfort and helped me enormously through the grieving process.

It was an assurance for me that it was well with my father's soul and somehow these words lifted me from a dark place of sorrow and gave me hope. I never quite saw death the same again.

So I give God all the praise, all the glory to know that He carried me through one of the most painful times of my life.

This was the beginning of me hearing the voice and inspiration of the Holy Spirit, which led to this book; 'Food for Your Soul.'

Introduction

THE Lord gave me a gift, he empowered me to hear these divine words and to put them on paper to feed the soul and sustain the spirit.

"Prayers and writings from a spiritually touched heart"

Spiritual wisdom and understanding comes from embracing God's Word in its entirety. The lord has blessed me with a special gift and I thank the Lord with all my heart. The written word is a powerful format for communication. God communicates to us through his word, but we must be spiritually in line with him in order to receive his word and to understand the contents of his word.

Prayers enhance our lives; it is the channel through which we are privileged to speak to God through Jesus our Lord and mediator.

The Lord has set wonderful examples for us of the way we must live in accordance with God's Word. Jesus has shown us kindness, pure and perfect love. He has also shown us wisdom and understanding and total unselfishness. No one has set a greater example than Jesus. He remained so humble, attending to the physical and spiritual needs of mankind. He did this whilst showing man how to worship God the father in spirit and truth. God our Father truly blessed mankind once again and gave us a chance to be redeemed from sin.

I thank you Father for the gift of your only begotten son Jesus Christ.

Who lived and died in order to save us from damnation and to give us eternal life in abundance.

So my brothers and sisters, take a prayer from this book each day to fill your soul with spiritual nourishment. Through praying and meditating upon the Lord, the soul will be nourished and strengthened. If the spiritual heart and soul of man gains no spiritual food it becomes weak and desolate and will affect the physical body.

By praying and reading the word of God we will gain a good spiritual heart for the Lord, and in turn our lives will be enhanced. Prayer is our divine channel for communication directly to God, so if we pray with a faithful pure heart our soul will receive spiritual food and we will be strengthened. If we do not pray with sincere hearts then our prayers will appear empty before God and we could not expect to hear from the Lord if we do not pray or pray without faith.

When we look upon the obstacles and problems we face in life we should not view them as mountains but we should rather view them as hills, because through faith the mountain will be only a hill, a grade in the landscape of life, which is easily climbed with Jesus by our side.

God is good and His mercy is everlasting

Thank you Lord

Amen

Food for the Soul

Each day I give thanks to the Lord God of Israel,
for without him I am nothing.
Lord the utterance of your name fills my soul with love.
I give thanks for your tender mercies. Let me humble myself before thee in thy presence, for you are Almighty God, from the beginning to everlasting. Man's life is like a shadow without your presence.
You give us the ability to sustain life through your awesome presence. My God you are so great, for you are pure without fault, your judgment is righteous and your timing is perfect.
Send your power dear Lord to enlighten me, for you have brought me out of darkness and into the light, for nothing can grow in darkness, but the spirit will flourish in the light. For your love comes from the light.
Lord bring me back to the place where I am meant to be!
It is the place where I see your perfect beauty, your tenderness, your truth and your mercy.
It is the place where I can adore and glorify you.
For you O'Lord are worthy to be praised.
Amen.

Food for Your Soul

Feed your Soul

*D*o not rely on your own understanding
but instead rely on God's Word.
For all knowledge and wisdom is in His Word.
Set your mind to meditate on the Lord, and open your heart
so that the Lord may enter.
For if your mind and heart meditate on the Lord
and is in one accord, then your soul shall be fed with spiritual food
and shall be satisfied.
Lift up yourself from this earthly plain and join the Lord through
meditation and prayer so that your soul shall flourish.
The body is easy to be fed but the soul is harder to feed.
Whatever is taken via the mouth is excreted after a while,
but whatever is taken unto the soul remains
and can only be removed by spiritual cleansing.
Therefore guard your soul even more than your body
and let only the Lord administer to your soul.
For it is the soul that needs God's salvation and redemption from sin.
The body is only a vessel, a shell which decays when we die.

Food for Your Soul

Therefore guard your soul well my brethren

for it is precious in the sight of God.

Praise the Lord forever more.

Amen

TO GOD BE THE GLORY

Food for Your Soul

Divine

Heavenly Father, divine spirit,
protects me from the perils of this world
for they are unseen to my eyes, but are always revealed to you.
Open my eyes Father so that I can see
the clear path you provide for me.
Send your angels to guide me, to hold me up if I should fall.
Let your Spirit be around me continually for this journey,
for I cannot travel without you.
Let me love my enemies,
that I may not keep any malice or hatred within my heart.
Let my heart be pure and undiluted,
filled with your love and grace with the power to forgive.
Give me your peace dear Lord.
My comforter, my God in whom I put all my trust.

Amen

TO GOD BE THE GLORY

Food for Your Soul

Thank You

Thank you Lord for the days that you give to me.
Thank you for yesterday.
Thank you for today.
Thank you for tomorrow.
Each breath I take, I know is precious.
Each step I take, please walk with me.
When I speak let me be watchful of the words I use.
Let the meditation of my heart be pure in truth, wisdom and love.
Let me please you in all the things I do,
because Father I need your guidance each and every day.

Amen

TO GOD BE THE GLORY

Food for Your Soul

Spirit

*M*y spirit cries out to you O'Lord.
Lead me and guide me in my entire daily task
Clear the path before me and remove all the obstacles,
for you know what is ahead of me.
Bless me O'Lord for I love you with all my heart, you are my treasure.
Lord I ask for pureness of heart, so that I can worship you
with power and strength in spirit and truth.

Amen
TO GOD BE THE GLORY

Food for Your Soul

Blessings

Lord you have blessed me out of the goodness of your heart.
It is an honour and a privilege to be blessed by your loving hands.
No longer do I have to worry about what will take place in my life
because I am truly blessed in every sense
and I know that whatever happens you are there.
Watch over me continually dear Lord each day and each night, I pray.
Your plan for me is my plan also,
for I need your guidance every step of the way,
whether the road is rocky or smooth,
Lord I know you are in control.
So I need you to show to me the path I must take
to my divine destination,
heavenly bound I am with you to hold my hand!
As you guide me all the way.

Amen

TO GOD BE THE GLORY

Food for Your Soul

A Father's Love

God has loved us from the beginning,
He made us in His own image.
Because of His great love,
He is able to forgive us when we are disobedient.
We grieved Him and angered Him,
yet He showed great mercy to us
when He sent His only begotten son Jesus Christ.
He lived, suffered on the cross for us, died and was resurrected.
He became our mediator, so that we could have a chance
to achieve eternal life, to live with Him in Glory.
How great is a father's love? He has surely shown us.
Therefore it should be with joy and honour that we praise Him
and worship Him with all our hearts
because no one loves us more than him.

Amen

TO GOD BE THE GLORY

Food for Your Soul

In Our Hearts

Whatever is in our heart is manifested in the words we speak,
so we need to guard the words which come from our mouths.
For by these words we align ourselves and commit ourselves
to ideas and beliefs.
Let the meditation of our hearts and minds be only of you dear Lord
and let our spirit flourish so that our hearts may be purified.
Lord you have the power to do all things.
Uplift us in our spirit and soul
so that we can worship in spirit and in truth.

Amen

TO GOD BE THE GLORY

Food for Your Soul

Joy

*M*y heart is glad and rejoices in thee.

Let your love surround me Lord,

that I may not be found wanting,

for you give me all I need and nothing is spared.

You have dealt with me bountifully Lord.

My heart desire is to praise you, to worship you, my redeemer, my God.

When I am low you lift me up and hold me in your arms.

When I am tired and cannot walk that extra mile you have carried me.

O' Lord you are so great!

I am left in awesome wonder at the love that you have for me.

You are the rock on which I stand for strength and comfort,

knowing in full assurance that you will be with me always.

Amen

TO GOD BE THE GLORY

Food for Your Soul

Changes

Nothing stays the same.
Look at the season's forever changing,
winter comes with a cold and misty feeling,
spring comes with new life,
summer comes with warmth and joy,
autumn comes with death and change.
These are the circles of life forever changing.
Within these seasons we experience God's great love,
for He created the seasons so that we can prepare ourselves
for the days and months ahead.
We see everything changing and we make ourselves ready
for the change.
The only sure thing that stays the same is God's love for us,
it never changes.
He loved us yesterday, today and tomorrow.
How great is our God!
Let us worship Him with all our heart and with all our might.
Amen

TO GOD BE THE GLORY

Food for Your Soul

Honour

Lord it is an honour to know you,
for if I did not know you then I would be in darkness.
You enrich my life in ways my tongue cannot tell!
When I am troubled and fear fills my heart, you are there.
With you by my side, fear has no hold over me.
It cannot cripple me for you have lifted me up
so I cannot fall.
You have held my hand so I cannot slip
for if the mountain seems too tall for me to climb
you will help me to climb it and I will reach the top.
If the road is rugged and winding you will make it smooth
and straighten the path so that I am able to walk.
Lord if the waters are deep you will be like a fisherman and cast your
net of salvation to catch me so that I will be saved.
May the glory, honour and praise be continually yours my God
and my lips shall sing of your goodness all day long
for there is none like you O Lord!
Amen

TO GOD BE THE GLORY

Food for Your Soul

Concern

Let me be kind in thoughts and deeds.

Let me be generous with kind words.

Let me think of others before I think of myself.

Let me be watchful for my brother and sister

even though they may not watch out for me.

Let my mind be consumed with generous thoughts for my brothers and sisters so that my spirit will not be selfish in thoughts and deeds, but flourish generously in the Lord.

Amen

TO GOD BE THE GLORY

Food for Your Soul

Thoughts of You

My mind is consumed with thoughts of you Lord.

Fill my thoughts with your wisdom, love and beauty

for you O'Lord are perfect in all your ways.

The power and glory that radiates from you is magnificent.

I will worship you and adore you in all your splendor,

for you know my needs before I ask

and when I ask you grant them freely.

Lord I pray, give me wisdom so that I may only ask for the things

that are really good for me,

not because my heart and mind desires it.

Wisdom is a gift from you,

which keeps me on the divine path of righteousness.

Amen

TO GOD BE THE GLORY

Food for Your Soul

Protect Me O'Lord

Lord you have taken up your shield to protect me. You have taken hold of your sword to defend me from my enemies. Lord you have sent your angels to lift me out of destruction
so that I will not fall from your presence.
Father you are so wonderful for you have shown me great love, patience and understanding.
I will give you the glory, honour and praise.
I will praise you O'Lord whilst I have the ability to communicate with you and sickness of the mind does not attack me.
Protect me I pray dear Lord so that I will be able to continue praising you all the days of my life until my earthly end and forever more. Thank you Lord

Amen

TO GOD BE THE GLORY

Food for Your Soul

Testimony of Love

The lord has loved me and blessed me.

The Lord has kept my feet from falling.

The lord has saved me from unseen dangers.

The Lord protected me from the evil that lurks day and night.

The lord has fed me when I was hungry.

The lord has clothed me and kept me from shame.

O'Lord I love you for your tender mercies

that you have extended to me.

I know Lord that I am truly precious in your sight.

I thank you with a grateful heart.

Amen

TO GOD BE THE GLORY

Food for Your Soul

Trust

The most high God radiates from the heavens in all his splendor,
for he is the Almighty creator of all things on earth and in heaven.
I will bow down and worship the God of Israel,
the God of my forefathers, for you O'Lord are worthy to be praised.
Truth and love radiates from you,
righteousness and justice are your tools.
Come to my aid Lord and vindicate me
from people who harbour malicious evil thoughts against me.
For you are my protector;
my guide in whom I put all my confidence.
O'Lord the glory and honour are yours
and I shall be victorious because I have put my trust in thee.

Amen

TO GOD BE THE GLORY

Food for Your Soul

The Way

The lord is the way and the truth and the life.
No one comes to the Father except through Him.
The Lord is the light which shines bright, warm and pure.
We are pulled towards the light
and need only to take that one step.
The Lord is the truth and he will never let us down.
All things that are of the Lord and come from the Lord
are true and pure, righteousness and justice belongs to Him.
The Lord is the way, I shall walk submitting myself to Him
to walk in obedience to His will.
He will restore me when I am weak
and make me strong when I feel faint hearted.
The Lord is the way, the truth and the life,
we must follow in order to come to the Father.
Praise be to my God for all His wonderful kindness,
His mercy endures forever and is eternal.
Amen

TO GOD BE THE GLORY

Food for Your Soul

Ministering Spirit

O'Lord knowledge and wisdom is a divine gift.
For not all things are revealed to man upon the plains of the earth,
only to your angels are your plans revealed.
In doing so your angels do you're bidding and minister to our needs.
For they are aware of all things concerning us.
Thank you Father for your ministering spirits who do your bidding.
When we exercise faith in you and speak your word,
worship you with sincere hearts,
your angels will attend to our needs on your behalf
and draw near to us to make our lives better.
But we must live the word that you have given to us,
for there is power in your word and the glory and victory are yours.
O'Lord give us knowledge and wisdom we pray,
so that we may fully understand all you wish us to know
and receive your divine purpose for our lives.

Amen

TO GOD BE THE GLORY

Food for Your Soul

Faith, Hope and Charity

Faith is a promise I have in the Lord
that I believe I shall have everlasting life
because Jesus suffered for me and died upon
the cross and was resurrected from death
so that I may have redemption for my sins.
Death has no power and has lost its' sting.
Through an act of selfless love O'Lord
I have a chance of everlasting life.
Thank you Lord.

Hope is a desire of the heart.
It is a feeling of joy which fills my soul,
to know how much you care for me.
I have a desire to walk with you all the days of my life
for I know you will fulfil all my hopes!.

Charity is love.
To be loved and to have love is the greatest gift.

Food for Your Soul

The love you have shown me Lord Jesus is the greatest gift of all
because you laid down your life for me
and became my mediator to Father God,
so that I may have the reward of everlasting life.
Thank you Lord for your kind deeds towards me. I will praise your
holy name for you are worthy to be praised.

Amen

TO GOD BE THE GLORY

Food for Your Soul

Nearer to my God

Put me not out of sight my God.
Let your presence be forever near me.
Draw near to me and I will draw near to thee.
Let me always be in your sight,
for when life becomes turbulent and unjust
I only have to ask and you will be by my side
to help me through the storms of life.
Though the waves bash against me
I will stand as firm as a rock,
for Lord you have strengthened me
and your power and glory surrounds me.
Joy fills my heart dear Lord to know that you love me
and will never leave me nor forsake me.
Draw nigh my God to me as I draw nigh to thee.

Amen

TO GOD BE THE GLORY

Food for Your Soul

Protect me my Lord

The Lord has comforted me and spoken softly to my soul.
Death and destruction lay either side of me.
O' Lord strengthen me I pray, bind death and destruction
and lift me from this perilous situation.
Send your angels Lord to lift me from this pit
and to set my feet upon solid ground,
for my heart desires to worship you
all the days of my life.
No power is greater than thee O'Lord, my everlasting God.
Therefore I ask you to make my path straight with righteousness,
my convictions strong and my faith unshakable.
Therefore I put my trust in you Lord,
for you are the God of righteousness, pure and true,
a marvel and a wonder to the nations.
Thank you for your loving kindness and mercies,
which you extend from generation to generation.

Amen

TO GOD BE THE GLORY

Food for Your Soul

My God is Great

The seeds of destruction planted against me will not flourish or grow
for in the name of Jesus, I bind all evil here on earth.
I ask that you release your legions of angels to perform your work,
so that I do not slip into darkness but remain in the light.
No army can defeat me, because the Lord leads me.
He takes me into battle and victory is mine.
My God is great because He is the true living God.
The God of Israel, the creator of Heaven and Earth
the Alpha and the Omega.
The God of life, whose love and power endures for all eternity.
He is awesome and wonderful.
It is my delight to call upon Him for
He is so mighty and faithful in all His ways.
My heart and soul shall praise you day and night,
as I think about how kind you are to me dear Lord.

Amen

TO GOD BE THE GLORY

Food for Your Soul

The Awesome Power of the Lord

O' Lord my God let me not doubt,
for your judgement is righteous and your timing is perfect.
I will charge into battle knowing that you are by my side
and insure knowledge that the victory will be mine
and the glory belongs to you O'Lord.
For with you by my side I am invincible.
No manner of evil can come near me or impede me
for my mission is Holy and the Lord is with me.
Deliver me speedily this day O'Lord
from fierce opposition for the glory belongs to you forever more.

Amen

TO GOD BE THE GLORY

Food for Your Soul

My Soul

The word of the Lord touches my soul
and brings conviction to my heart.
I have succumbed to his voice, to his power and his will.
His voice hovered on the void and darkness became light
for the Almighty God has spoken "What will be, will be".
He commands the sun, the moon, the stars,
the rain, the snow, the wind.
All the elements listen for the word of His command.
Men should listen for the word of His command also,
but sometimes they do not hear when the voice of the Lord speaks
to them they are like deaf men who live in silence.
Dear Lord please keep my heart connected to your Spirit,
so that I will hear your voice and so speak your language,
understand your wisdom,
adhere to your word and be obedient to your voice.

Amen

TO GOD BE THE GLORY

Food for Your Soul

The Lord is Good

God is good and his mercy endures forever,

His patience is bountiful.

Praise to my God for his infinite wisdom

and understanding towards me.

The seasons will come and go, and the earth is moved to change.

The seasons are given to us as a time of preparation.

Lord please bless me with a bountiful harvest

of spiritual understanding and wisdom.

So brethren I say unto you, let us be watchful,

diligent and prepare our heart so that when the Lord returns

we shall not be found wanting,

but will be ready for him to receive us into his eternal kingdom.

Praise be to the Lord God of Israel for all eternity.

Amen

TO GOD BE THE GLORY

Food for Your Soul

The Essence of the Lord

The essence and the beauty of the Lord are within us.
The beauty of the Lord is manifested in us
through prayer and meditation upon the word of God.
Let us use the essence of the Lord in all we do.
Let the works of our hands be a testimony
to the power and glory of God.
Let our hearts be clean and pure.

Let us not harbour malice, contempt, deceit, or hatred in our hearts.
Let us be watchful of the words we speak
so that we do not defile ourselves by our own mouths.

For if we speak negatively
then negativity will be manifested in our lives.
Therefore my brethren let our thoughts be pure, clean, and positive,
so that goodness flows and is manifested in our lives.

The Lord wants to bestow upon us the treasures of a long life
filled with joy, happiness and love.

Food for Your Soul

Let our hearts and mouths continually
praise the Lord God of Israel all the days of our lives.

Amen

TO GOD BE THE GLORY

Food for Your Soul

A Thankful Heart

The Lord has anointed my head with oil
and brought me from low ebb.
He restored my soul and my countenance returned to me.
My God is truly great, for in my adversity He thought of me
and came to my aid.
I am nothing without his presence.
Praise be to the Lord for His mercy and love
He has extends towards me.
I will praise thee in humble adoration
and my tongue shall continually say
how great and precious is thy love!
I thank you Lord with all my heart.
Let the glory honour and praise be yours
all the days of my life and forever more.

Amen

TO GOD BE THE GLORY

Food for Your Soul

The Road

A man wondered endlessly from one day to the next,
from one month to the next, from one year to the next,
without aim, without direction, without love and compassion.
One night he fell into a deep sleep,
he dreamt that he was walking without direction,
lost and confused, he found himself on a winding road.
As he walked along this road he noticed
that parts of the road were smooth and easy to walk on,
but he also noticed that several times he fell
because of obstacles that appeared from nowhere
which hindered him as he walked.
The man came to a crossroad and became even more confused
because he could not decide which road to take.
As he stood at the crossroad lost and confused
he heard a voice, from behind him say;
"My son are you lost?"
The man answered without a thought and said;
"Yes I am".
A moment passed and he heard the voice say;

Food for Your Soul

"Which road would you like to take?"

The man replied;

"The road that is smooth and safe, that has no danger or obstacles."

The voice replied;

"The roads that you see in front of you are the same,

and they present the same obstacles,

but if you will have faith and believe in me,

I shall walk with you and uphold you

so that you shall not fall and I will strengthen you on this journey.

For even as you wandered aimlessly throughout the years past

I have always been with you, lifting you up each time you fell.

Even on this path to this crossroad,

it was me who picked you up when you fell."

The man fell to the ground and began to weep.

As he wept he felt a hand upon his shoulder,

and the same comforting voice saying;

"Why do you weep my son?"

and the man replied;

"Because you have thought of me Lord,

even when I did not think of you".

The voice replied;

Food for Your Soul

"My son you are my child

and a Father always cares for his children."

As the man heard this, his countenance changed

and joy filled his soul. He stood up, turned to the Lord and said;

"Father will you walk with me on this journey?"

The lord replied;

"Yes my son."

Amen

TO GOD BE THE GLORY

Food for Your Soul

Power

The power of God protects me from unseen dangers
for I have kept my covenant with the Lord;
therefore he will never leave me.
My heart is filled with joy as I walk with the Lord,
knowing that nothing can attack me,
"I am immune and covered under His wings!"
The Lord is my protector and my deliverer,
so I ask, "Lord send your angels to bear me up"
please let their presence be around me.
Father I thank you with all my heart
for I am not alone and fear has no power over me.
Joy and hope fills the space where loneliness and fear once lived,
because I know that my heart belongs to you Lord Jesus.
Your promise of everlasting life captivates my soul
and my spirit dwells at peace knowing that you are near.

Hallelujah, Amen
TO GOD BE THE GLORY

Food for Your Soul

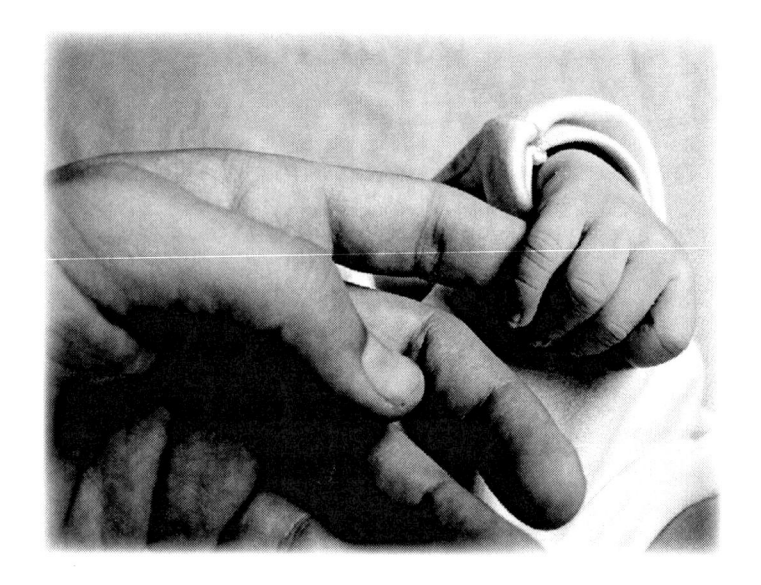

The Circle of Life

The light is so bright I cannot see.
The noise is so loud it deafens me.
I cannot speak for I do not have a language.
My mother holds me in her arms and cuddles me to her bosom.
My Father leans over me and joy fills his heart
for the Lord has given them a special gift.
He has blessed them, and multiplied them.
The years roll on and I grow tall and strong.
I gain knowledge and understanding of the world around me.

Food for Your Soul

The youthful years are now, behind and manhood now beckons me.
I take a wife and raise a family of my own
and now God has blessed me with my own special gift.
The same joy my father and Mother felt, I now feel!
I am now in the prime of life
living in the purpose of my creators design.
The years just flew by as if in a blink of an eye.
I grow weak as the strength of my youthful years subside
and memories fade.
I start to bend like a weeping willow tree.
My gait becomes unsteady, my eyes grow dim.
My speech and thoughts become slow
and my hearing is not as sharp as it use to be.
Now I come to the end of my journey.
I look back at my life and the years past,
it is good I knew the Lord
and listened to him when he spoke to me.
For the Lord has blessed me abundantly
and given me a promise of everlasting life.
Now I am old and sick, the Lord will always think of me
for He knows what is in my heart.

Food for Your Soul

As I look towards my final sleep;

"thank you Lord for all your blessings,

your tender mercies and unfailing love."

May the glory, honour and praise

be yours Lord all the days of my life and forever more.

Amen

TO GOD BE THE GLORY

Food for Your Soul

Glory

*M*y Father sits on his throne in heaven.
He stretches out His hands
and opens his arms so that I can run to Him
for comfort when I am in distress.
He gives me peace and shelters me from the storms of life.
He protects me and fights my battles
because He is the Almighty God of Israel
whose love endures forever and his promise is faithful and true.
All my faith and hope is in you O'Lord.
You will make me stand firm
because you have made my foundations strong.
Continually strengthen me O'Lord
so that I may grow in faith, because the power and
the glory belongs to you always.

Amen

TO GOD BE THE GLORY

Food for Your Soul

The Future

$\mathcal{D}$o not search for what is lost

for what is lost is gone it is in the past and cannot be found.

Look to the future which lays ahead,

hold onto the Lord and He will help you through.

For the future is bright and filled with light.

Let the past stay the past for what is done is done,

it can hold no reward for you.

It is a time already spent!

Let the Lord show you the way,

a future filled with love and promise

where he guides us by his loving hands today and always.

Amen

TO GOD BE THE GLORY

Food for Your Soul

Treasures

I do not search for the treasures of this world
for they are shallow and empty
and can only give me pleasure for a short time.
Instead I search for the treasures stored up in Heaven
which the Lord has promised me.
They are the treasures of everlasting life
and forgiveness of my sins.
These are the greatest treasures a man can search for.
Not silver or gold, for silver and gold will fade over time
but the Lord's promise is eternal
and everlasting enduring all generations.

Amen

TO GOD BE THE GLORY

Food for Your Soul

The Miracle of God

O Lord as I looked upon the night skies
I saw the beauty of your hands at work.
The moon and the stars which shine so bright
the source of its enduring power
comes from your creative hands.
Even in darkness you gave us light,
so that we do not stumble or fall,
but are able to see and be upright.
It is such a beautiful sight to behold Lord
I see your unconditional love and mercy,
pure and kind, never wavering or standing still,
but growing all the time.
Lord I received your gift of salvation,
which spared me from destruction,
redeeming me from my sins
and giving me the opportunity of everlasting life.
For in you my life is complete.
For I am joyful in your presence,

Food for Your Soul

to behold your beauty; splendor and mercy.

For Lord you are truly wonderful!

I declare that the Lord is worthy to be praised

all the days of my life and forevermore.

Thank you Lord.

Amen

TO GOD BE THE GLORY

Food for Your Soul

A Wedding Prayer

As I walked the pathway of life,
the Lord led you to me and joined our hearts together.
Today we became one as he joined us in holy matrimony.
To love, honour, cherish and obey.
To love you in spirit and deeds.
To care for you at all times.
To cherish you is to hold you dear
and acknowledge that you are precious
more than silver and gold.

Food for Your Soul

To honour you is to appreciate all that you do for me,
to respect you emotionally and physically.
To obey is to put the Lord before us,
to love, to honour, to cherish him even more than ourselves.
For the Lord our God has joined us together
and shall keep us together.
When the road gets rough the Lord will clear the path
and remove the obstacles.
When we are tired the Lord will carry us
and sustain us throughout our lives together,
for we shall always put the Lord first
as we take this journey together
and He shall be our focus, the centre of our joy!
As we share our lives together.

Amen

TO GOD BE THE GLORY

Food for Your Soul

Hope

Where there is hope there is faith and trust.
The belief and aspirations of our desires
are fully realised in the Lord.
My hope is in the Lord, my deliverer.
For Jehovah is a faithful God.
If He says, "I will", then He will.
He is generous and ever sure,
faithful to His word and to all who believe in Him.
Without my God I am nothing,
I would be like the dust upon the ground,
but the Lord has shaped me and moulded me.
I am a new creature in Him.
He sustains me all the days of my life.
The Lord is mighty and able to deliver.
I cry out to him, He will hear my voice;
for it is He who has made me.
I am a child of God,
and I shall not depart from my Fathers presence,

Food for Your Soul

but shall keep all his ways and walk in his paths.
O Lord my God you looked upon me with mercy
in the days of my youth and
in old age when I acquired a little more wisdom.
For I have remembered all your kindness
and your love towards me.
I shall praise you all the days of my life,
my Lord, my God, my redeemer.
Hallelujah

Amen
TO GOD BE THE GLORY

Food for Your Soul

Set My Spirit Free

God has set my spirit free.

Yes He set my spirit free.

From the cares and tribulations of this world,

He set my spirit free.

I soared to great heights as He elevated me,

for He has broken the bonds of sin and set me free.

What shall I do with my new found freedom?

I shall serve the Lord with all my heart, now I am free!

The Lord has shown me great love in the salvation he has given me

because the Lord did not create me to be bound

by the chains of sin.

He created me with a free spirit,

which desires to serve and worship him with joy and delight.

So thank you Lord for my free spirit

and the salvation you gave me.

Father lead me on your path of righteousness

and teach me all truth as I live for you each day.

TO GOD BE THE GLORY

Food for Your Soul

Spiritual Peace

The Lord has set my spirit free
and I am no longer earth bound but heavenly bound.
As I pray, uplift my spirit Lord
so that I may be enlightened and acquire the knowledge
and wisdom you desire me to have.
For my spirit belongs to you Lord for all eternity.
Lord continually cleanse my spirit of all impurities
and let your Holy Spirit dwell with my spirit
in perfect harmony submitting to His authority.
Give me your perfect speech the heavenly language,
which transcends my understanding but edifies my spirit.
Lift me Lord to another level in mind, spirit and soul.

Amen

TO GOD BE THE GLORY

Food for Your Soul

A Special Sight

A prayer was once prayed for me.
The person prayed;
"Lord remove the scales from her eyes so that she can see."
The Lord answered the prayer hastily,
and the scales were dusted from my eyes.
As though He blew upon my eyes and the scales dropped to the floor.
I opened my eyes, and I could see a whole new world,
where everything looked different.
I became wise and prudent especially in matters of the heart.
Wisdom and knowledge were the gifts the Lord
bestowed upon me and I saw that the Lord truly loved me
even though he knew my fault and knew I was not perfect.
As time went by and revelations came to me,
I knew that I was blessed by the Lord opening my eyes,
and giving me a new sight.
I also knew that my life would never be the same again.
In time I gained strength and became stronger than ever before.
I shall praise the Lord and thank him for the sight he gave me,

Food for Your Soul

because I have gained so much through this vision.

I now have understanding and wisdom.

Lord I thank you with a humble heart

because as I look back at my life,

I don't know where I would be without your love and protection

for you have never forsaken me.

You protected me from dangers, which surrounded me

and drew me out of calamities that would have befallen me.

My new sight has given me visions of your love and your power.

For your judgement is perfect and flawless.

Thanks be to the Lord for ever more.

Amen and Amen

TO GOD BE THE GLORY

Food for Your Soul

The Lord Thinks of Me

I am delighted to know

that the Lord has thought of me throughout my life.

The Lord has shielded me from disasters, which came upon me,

and lifted me out of situations that I could not manage.

He has laid his hands upon me in such a wonderful way!

The Lord has done this because I have called upon him.

It is pleasing to me to see how the Lord thinks of me.

The glory of the Lord has been upon me

and I have seen the beauty of his love.

As he lifted me up towards the light,

it shone so bright that my eyes could hardly contain the beauty,

joy and warmth I felt.

I will praise His name continually,

for the Lord God of Israel is truly worthy to be praised,

to be glorified, to be magnified and honoured all the days of my life.

Amen

TO GOD BE THE GLORY

Food for Your Soul

The Yoke and Light

The glory of the Lord surrounds me and fills my heart with joy.
The burden of this world is reduced by the Spirit of the Lord.
The Lord has lifted the yoke from my shoulders so that I can walk
with strength and without difficulty.
"Thank you Lord."
The Lord is magnificent and generous in his love towards me.
He lifted me out of disasters and prevented my enemies
laying hold of me.
He has given his angels charge over me,
to protect me and to keep me safe at all cost.
The Lord is with me I shall not be afraid!
The Lord is Holy, pure and righteous, all his ways are proven.
I shall not depart from the Lord,
for it is He who keeps me.
I am alive by his will and blessed by him.
My God is truly great,
and with a heart of gratitude I shall worship the Lord
all the days of my life.

Food for Your Soul

Glory and praise to the Lord God of Israel for his wonderful works and loving kindness, now and forevermore.

Amen and Amen

TO GOD BE THE GLORY

Food for Your Soul

The Journey

The Lord does not slumber,

but watches continually over me;

because I am precious in his sight.

For I know that the Lord loves me.

Therefore with all my might,

I shall follow the righteous path he has laid for me.

I shall not depart from the path for He is with me every step of the way.

He strengthens me and he gives me vitality and boldness,

to perform the task that seems too hard for me to achieve.

I have put my trust in the Lord

and know in full assurance that he is with me on this journey

and all the days of my life.

Lord I thank you for being my shepherd,

may the glory be yours forever more.

Amen

TO GOD BE THE GLORY

Food for Your Soul

The Mercy of the Lord

I shall clear my heart of the injustice and hurt done to me.

For the Lord thought of me and lifted me out of the hands

of my enemies, so that they could not lay hold of me

or bind me in the chains of destruction.

My God is awesome for he thought of me,

and extended his kind mercies towards me.

I shall follow the Lord for He is righteous and merciful.

He has always thought of me,

so I ask dear Lord; "keep me near"

in your thoughts my rock my saviour.

I depend on you, without you I am like an empty shell upon a beach,

which the tide pushes backwards and forwards.

Fill my vessel Lord with your Spirit,

so that I can worship you in spirit and in truth.

Amen

TO GOD BE THE GLORY

Food for Your Soul

Guard My Mouth, Guard My Thoughts

Lord let me be mindful of others and watchful

of the words which I speak,

for there is power in the words I speak and the thoughts I harbour.

So let my thoughts and words be pure.

Lord let your essence be in my words as I think and speak.

Lord let my words be kind and true, not hateful or malicious,

because a word is a tool.

It can sooth a broken heart, mend a broken friendship,

yet it can also cut into a person like a sharp knife.

So let me be watchful of the thoughts I think,

the words I speak and guard my mouth.

Let my words always be filled with grace

just like the Lord I honour and serve.

Amen

TO GOD BE THE GLORY

Food for Your Soul

Heal My Body and Uplift my soul

Almighty God I call upon you to heal my body,
to take away this vile affliction which is crippling my body.
Lay your hands upon me Lord
and I shall be delivered from this affliction.
You are powerful and great, the God of Israel and of all generations.
Even when I am in great pain and distress,
I shall always call upon the Lord,
for your promise is faithful and true.
For you have said you will never leave me nor forsake me.
Make haste my God and rescue me from the sorrow
and destruction that surrounds me.
Send your angels to watch over me dear Lord
and to spare me from this distress.
I am your faithful servant and Lord you are my master.
My reward is in your love. Blessed be the Lord for eternity.
Amen

TO GOD BE THE GLORY

Food for Your Soul

Protect Me Lord 2

Lord help me to live up to your expectations

and not man's expectations.

Shield me from negative influences

and from people who mean me harm.

They have nothing good for me, and they are not of your fold.

They lie and cheat, devising ways to deceive me,

but I am protected from them,

because I believe in the righteousness and glory of the Lord.

I know that the Lord will protect me from evil men

and their devices.

They cannot come near me

for his angels are set to watch over me day and night.

The Lord hides me in the secret place of his holy tabernacle.

I will not depart from Almighty God.

I will adhere to him for he is awesome and wonderful,

righteous and pure.

It is a privilege to know the Lord, for He has taken me from darkness

Food for Your Soul

and removed the veil from my eyes so that I can see.

O' Lord I thank you for you are truly great,

my heart and soul belongs to you forever.

Amen

TO GOD BE THE GLORY

Food for Your Soul

Lift My Spirit

The Lord has lifted my spirit
and removed the dark clouds from over my head.
He sent beams of light which lit the path in front me!
Father you have always loved me.
Let me not hesitate, but let me walk upright and strong in faith.
With you by my side how can I fail!
My victory is assured I will be triumphant in battle and strife.
You O Lord are my God and the glory belongs to you,
for you created the Heavens and the Earth
and blew life into all creatures.
My God you are truly awesome, in all your ways.
Lord give me wisdom and strength;
please send the precious Holy Spirit
to comfort me and to lead me into all truth.

Amen

TO GOD BE THE GLORY

Food for Your Soul

My Father Watches Over Me

I have called upon the Lord throughout my life,
during my trails, tribulations and turmoil's
he has always been merciful faithful and kind.
He has answered me when I called upon him,
for the Lord is watchful and mindful of me.
The Lord has steered me away from calamities,
destructions and death.
The Lord has blessed me with life more abundant in him!
Lord, Thank you for thinking of me, for never leaving me.
My heart fills with joy and delight
when I think of what the Lord has done for me.
I know that that you love me unconditionally and without measure!
Lord I pray let me dwell in your house all the days of my life
and let my lips continually praise your holy name,
for you are worthy to be praised.
Amen

TO GOD BE THE GLORY

Food for Your Soul

Strong Faith

Lord you have surpassed all my expectations of how you care for me.

You think of me when I do not think of myself.

You remember me at all times.

The Holy Spirit fills my heart with His presence

and I am uplifted from the depths of grief and sorrow.

Lord you are so precious to me,

for you have made my foundation strong.

You have placed my feet upon a rock and I shall not be moved.

I shall adhere to your commands

and listen to your words diligently all the days of my life.

Your word feed my soul and are my source of comfort to me;

they have sustained me in perilous times and lifted me from sorrow.

Lord bless me with knowledge, wisdom, understanding and patience.

For I desire not to stray from the path of righteousness,

which you have laid for me for it is a divine path

and you will be by my side as you have promised.

Strengthen me O Lord

so that I'm able to perform the task you have set before me.

You are my God whom I serve,

Food for Your Soul

and on whom I wait all the days of my life.

Praise be to Lord forever.

Amen

TO GOD BE THE GLORY

Food for Your Soul

A Clear Path

I shall not be distracted nor impeded from the divine path laid for me.

The Lord my God watches over me.

He keeps me safe, nourishes and nurtures me in strength,

so that I may walk this path.

I shall call upon the Lord always

for I have put my trust in him.

The Lord will answer me because He knows the desires of my heart.

Lord, thank you for your love, which you have bestowed upon me.

Thank you for your promise of everlasting life

and your mercy which prevails.

I shall stand steadfast in my faith

for Lord you are righteous and awesome in all your ways.

Amen

TO GOD BE THE GLORY

Food for Your Soul

The Path of Life

As I walk the pathways of life many events have taken place.
There have been times of great happiness, joy, elations and celebrations,
at births at weddings, and all of life's success.
But there have also been times when it would seem that the paths
I have travelled have been so rough.
Times filled with great sorrow, grief, pain and despair; relationship
breakdowns and the bereavement of a loved one so dear to my heart.
Such times are painful to remember,
so I place them to rest in the past with your help dear Lord.
As I look back at my life one thing has remained constant
and as never changed, your love for me Lord has kept me throughout
and I have been truly blessed by your presence.
So I thank you Lord with a grateful heart
as I remember your wonderful kindness and your mercy towards me.

Amen

TO GOD BE THE GLORY

Food for Your Soul

Angels

O Lord your angels surround me on every side.

They bear me up in their hands and I am lifted from the pit

of destruction of sorrow and calamity.

They place my feet upon the rock of salvation

so no harm can come near me.

For you O Lord have been gracious to me

by giving your angels charge over me so that I will be safe.

Lord I feel the presence of your love

and it touches the inner chambers of my heart.

I am at peace through your protection for I know I am not alone.

Lord I pray,

"Be forever near me throughout my life."

I need your presence continually

because the gift of salvation is so precious to me.

Amen

TO GOD BE THE GLORY

Food for Your Soul

My God Knows Me

O Lord you have always known me, from the beginning of time,
even before I was created and moulded by your loving hands.
When I was only a concept in your mind, you knew me Lord.
How then could I ever depart from your loving presence?
I could not!
For your love has carried me Lord and preserved my life.
You are my father and I am your child.
I shall be attentive and obedient to all your ways and commandments.
I shall not depart from your ways for you O Lord
have always been faithful to me, I am nourished by your presence.
Lord you have strengthened my body and mind so that I am strong,
my enemies cannot defeat me.
Purify my thoughts Lord at all times
and clarify the deeds which you desire me to perform,
let your perfect will be done.
For you are my father, my life is in your hands.
I shall wait upon you Lord all days of my life.
Amen

TO GOD BE THE GLORY

Food for Your Soul

I Know the Lord, Knows Me

My mind is filled with joy and excitement when I hear your name.

Lord you are acquainted with all my ways,

I am not like a stranger to you.

I have called upon the Lord and he has answered me.

I am blessed by him.

When I go into the house of the Lord,

I am not a visitor for the Lord knows me and I know the Lord.

He welcomes me with open arms.

I will sup with the Lord and He will sup with me

because He is my Father.

Lord let your presence be in my life continually

for I will give you the glory forever more.

Your mercy endures from generation to generation,

for you are flawless in all your ways

and your favour is without measure.

I am blessed by your presence

as I continue to live a life of worship to you.

Thank you Lord.

TO GOD BE THE GLORY

Food for Your Soul

The Lord Protects Me

When sickness and infirmity tries to pull me down,
the Lord will lift me up.
The Lord has given his angels assignments for the battle
I shall not be defeated by the plans of the enemy.
My God will crush the arrows of destruction under my feet
and pound them into oblivion .
The Lord will nourish my soul and make my body strong.
The Lord will drive away my adversaries
so that all their plans come to nought.
I am kept safe and secure in his presence.
My faith and hope rest in the knowledge of how mighty the Lord is,
"Jehovah Nissi is your name."
I shall not be moved because the Lord is my keeper.
I shall delight myself in His presence
and receive all his blessings.
I praise you Lord, I magnify you my king, my almighty saviour.

Amen

TO GOD BE THE GLORY

Food for Your Soul

Understanding

O Lord my mind is perplexed by the things I see
and cannot understand.
I pray that you will give me wisdom and knowledge.
If it is possible to change a bad or negative situation
to a good outcome with your guidance and assistance, let it be so.
Let me not rely on my own understanding of the situation
but let me rely on you.
Let me not be judgemental of other people,
for judgement belongs to you.
Lord you know each of our hearts,
when we stand together in your assembly.
Whenever the door knocks and someone is seeking you,
let us gladly open it and welcome them in,
for the blessings of your kingdom belongs to them also.
O Lord let me be forthright in spirit,
kind in words and deeds towards my brethren.
If we are united, we are stronger because love binds us together.
Bless all who believe in you O Lord
and those who do not know you.

Food for Your Soul

I pray that you will open their hearts
to accept you and let their eyes behold your glory.

Amen

TO GOD BE THE GLORY

Food for Your Soul

Reassurance in the Lord

My lips shall forever sing thy praise O Lord,
draw near to me my God as I shall always call upon thee.
As I walk this road I shall not stumble.
As I climb this mountain I shall not slip.
When deep waters surround me it shall not over take me
for you are the God I serve,
you shall lift me from perpetual dangers that lurk around me.
What my eyes cannot see is revealed to me by the Holy Spirit.
Every breath I take is because you have blessed me with life.
I shall not be wasteful with the years which you have given me
for time is precious, more than silver and gold.
Shower me dear Lord with your eternal blessings
and bless also my generations to come.
Your word is mighty, true, pure and kind.
Your promise is everlasting and you have never failed me yet!
I shall not ponder, nor waver but grow strong in faith,
secure in your love.
Lord I ask for your continual guidance in my life.

Food for Your Soul

I thank you Lord for your love and patience towards me.
My lips shall continually praise your Holy name all the days of my life.

Amen

TO GOD BE THE GLORY

Food for Your Soul

Deliverance 1

When sorrow and despairs fills my heart
and sadness consumes me,
I can do nothing else but look to the Lord my God for deliverance.
For I have called upon the Lord, yesterday, today and always.
He has heard me when I called and has answered me.
The Lord has rescued me from dyer situations
which were too great for me to handle.
He is truly awesome in all his ways,
for he removes the obstacles that the enemy lays.
The Lord has strengthened me for He is strong in my weakness.
The Lord loves me for he has proven his love for me so many times.
O Lord I thank you for your enduring love and for the blessings
you have bestowed upon me.
I shall always praise you and worship you forever more.
Great is the Lord and worthy to be praised from this generation
to the next for eternity in Heaven and on earth.
Hallelujah, Hallelujah.

Food for Your Soul

God's Love

The seasons come and go and life around us changes,
but one thing that remains constant in my life is God's love for me.
God's love never changes, it endures throughout time and it is unfailing.
God's love is the same yesterday, today and tomorrow.
God is generous towards me with his love
and he does not measure His love in portions
because his love is pure and unconditional.
O Lord my God, I shall love with passion,
with a pureness of heart, mind and spirit.
Let it be enduring as your love is not measured by the seasons.
You are my father who created me with loving hands
and fashioned the days for me.
O Lord I shall spend my days wisely
for time has a limit and it is precious.
Let my life be useful to you Lord and I shall be contented.
Your presence in my life gives me hope and joy.
My soul is filled with your love,
for you have poured out your blessings upon me.

Food for Your Soul

Uplift me always Lord, place me before thy presence
for you have made my feet to stand firm upon a rock
and made my foundation unshakable.
Praises be to the Lord God of Israel
for He has never forgotten me and his love never changes.

Amen

TO GOD BE THE GLORY

Food for Your Soul

My Life

My life is like a story book
I know of the beginning, some of the middle but I do not know the end,
for my times are not in my hands, it is in the Lord's hands.
Father I am assured through your love and promise of everlasting life.
So let me not stray from your divine purpose which is set for me.
The reward in you is great, it is greater than any earthly riches,
I cannot compare it!
O Lord I shall use my time wisely to seek you willingly
and be prudent as I walk.
Remove the stumbling blocks and clear the pathway dear Lord.
Open my eyes to the things you desire to reveal to me.
Give me strength so that I will be strong,
for I am on a mission for my God.
Praise the Lord for his mercies,
for his compassion and for his love.

Amen

TO GOD BE THE GLORY

Food for Your Soul

Heal Me Lord

O Lord my God, heal my body I pray
take away this vial rampant disease which ravishes my flesh.
Let your spirit enter my body,
so that this disease cannot dwell here anymore
for I have put my trust in you, the God of my forefathers.
This disease came upon me like a thief in the night.
It attacked me without cause, it clings to my flesh
and tries to bind me with its chains of destruction.
O Lord my God my soul cries out to you, I am faint hearted.
Lord remove this disease cleanse my body
and strengthen my soul for I have put my trust in thee.
Lord I ask, lift me up from this bed of sickness
and change my countenance.
The Lord has done marvellous works by his hands,
my trust in him shall be rewarded.
Pain and sorrow must leave this body
in the precious name of Jesus my Redeemer.
For the Lord has cleansed me and driven this disease away.

Food for Your Soul

It cannot dwell here anymore.

Praise be to my God for he is mighty, awesome, righteous and pure.

Hallelujah

Amen

TO GOD BE THE GLORY

Food for Your Soul

The Bounty

The Lord has dealt with me bountifully and has blessed me abundantly.
The Lord has opened doors which were shut to me
and shut the doors that I could not close.
The Lord is wonderful, without him I would have no hope
or purpose to my life.
The Lord has never abandoned me to the woes of this world,
because he stands beside me.
I am strengthened to face the dangers
and obstacles that may come towards me.
The Lord stretches his hands towards me
and I hold onto him.
He opens his arms and folds them around me, and I am comforted.
O Lord my God you are so wonderful to me, you cannot be compared.
For your glory and handy works are all around me.
My heart delights in the beauty of your holiness.
I shall forever call upon the Lord God of Israel
for you have always been faithful to me.
Your presence in my life has given me hope and joy beyond this world.
Lord you are magnificent!

Food for Your Soul

and worthy to be praised to be glorified all the days of my Life.

Amen

TO GOD BE THE GLORY

Food for Your Soul

Deliverance 2

*P*raise be to my God
for he has lifted me out of calamities that came my way.
The Lord has plucked me from the jaws of the lion
who was about to attack me.
The Lord has snatched me from the hands of my enemies
who seek to destroy me.
I have called upon the Lord and he has answered me.
He has not delayed in coming to my aid,
but he has made haste to deliver me speedily
and has poured out his love upon me bountifully.
I am therefore honoured and delighted
to see how my God has dealt with me.
I thank you Lord with all my heart,
for you looked at me and saw all my needs
and nothing was too great for you to do for me.
My lips shall continually praise you
and worship you all the days of my life.
"Holy Spirit I invite you to come and abide with me in perfect harmony,

Food for Your Soul

as I surrender all to you in Jesus name."

Hallelujah Hallelujah

Amen

TO GOD BE THE GLORY

Food for Your Soul

Eat Drink and Be Merry

Eat, drink and be merry.

Look to the future and not the past

for the past is behind you and is gone.

Whereas the future is in front of you and is filled with hope.

Only God knows the future,

so look to the Lord and say to him.

"Father protect me, guide me,"

and carry me through the trials and tribulations

that may lie ahead of me.

The Lord's hand is there reaching out to you to help the rest of the way.

So put all your trust in the Lord,

for He shall carry you home to glory,

He will not leave you half way.

Hold on tight to the Lord,

for the road may be rough but he will carry you,

because you have given your heart to him without hesitation.

He will never fail you, nor will He leave you

for He is a faithful God who keeps his promises.

Praise be to the Lord for you are the Alpha and the Omega.

Amen

Food for Your Soul

The Presence of the Lord

I feel the presence of the Lord within my life.
The things around me that seemed so important,
now seem unimportant to me.
My focus is on the Lord!
In my youth I made mistakes and learned along the way.
In my later years I became more prudent and wise through
the wisdom and knowledge the Lord gave me.
The scales of naivety which covered my eyes were removed
by the Lord through prayer and I was blessed with a new vision
and fresh revelations.
My journey has been long and hard to this point in my life,
but as I look back at my life, I realise that during the trials
and tribulations, the years of sadness and tears,
the years I called the lost years, I was not alone.
The Lord was with me throughout, every step of the way.
I need not ask or wonder if the Lord loves me,
for I know with all my heart that he loves me
more than words could express.

Food for Your Soul

So I thank you Lord with a grateful heart,

for without your love, I don't know where I would be.

The Lord has truly blessed me, time and time again.

Thank you Lord

Amen.

TO GOD BE THE GLORY

Food for Your Soul

He Moulds My Life

The joy of the Lord is in the beauty of the Lord
where my strength abides. There is no decay,
no corruptions in his promise for his word is perfect
and his ways are proven, his promise is everlasting and sure.
The Lord is faithful in all his ways and perfect in his timing.
The Lord is impeccable in all matters.
He prunes away the things from us that are no good
and replaces them with newness,
meaningfulness and goodness.

Food for Your Soul

As a Father looking at his child,

He wants only the very best for that child

and as the Father, he knows what is best.

So let us forever look to our Father for guidance,

protection and love, in all matters

so that we do not stray from his righteous path.

Let us love and adore the Lord who created all things

in Heaven and on earth. For the Lord is mighty and truly worthy.

Let us praise and worship him all the days of our lives.

Amen.

Food for Your Soul

Divine Spirit

O Lord wash away from me everything which is revealed to be unclean,

so that I will be pure in your sight.

The evil that lurks around cannot enter my soul

or my dwelling, for thou art with me.

I am protected by God, whose power is infinite and awesome.

The Lord has despatched Angels to protect my physical body

and guard my spirit.

My soul is comforted by their presence,

divine ministering spirits sent by the Lord.

I would be lost had I not believed in the Lord

and the promise that he made to me.

The Lord has quenched my thirst, fed my soul and I am at peace,

waiting for his eternal kingdom.

Praise be to the Lord for all his kindness and mercies.

Amen.

TO GOD BE THE GLORY

Food for Your Soul

Commitment

*M*y heart desires to worship the Lord in spirit and in truth,
in mind, body, and soul with clarity,
not half hearted, but fully committed.
So Lord I place myself before thee,
as a child who needs continual guidance and protection.
Lord I ask please walk with me
for I need your comforting Spirit, wisdom,
protection and love every step of the way!
Let me be nourished and sustained by your presence
each and every day, and I shall always be thankful,
praising you all the days of my life.

Amen.

TO GOD BE THE GLORY

Food for Your Soul

Great Love

The Lord loves me this I know to be true!
The Lord has never left me, nor forsaken me.
I have slipped and fallen numerous times
but the Lord has always lifted me up.
I have prayed today and received my blessings tomorrow,
that's how much the Lord loves me.
Obstacles that have been placed in my midst,
as been removed by the Lord.
The Lord has opened doors of opportunity for me,
and has turned around situations in my favour.
I am amazed to see the awesome wonder and goodness of my God,
to see just how much he loves and cares for me.
The love of God touches my spirit and I am filled with tears of joy
and happiness, to see how the Lord loves me.
Thank you Father for your loving kindness and tender mercies,
for continually loving me.
When I was heartbroken and did not love myself
you loved me and lifted me up to stand
tall with strength in your presence.

Food for Your Soul

You have given me a new vitality for life.

I love the Lord God of Israel because he has always loved me.

Amen.

TO GOD BE THE GLORY

Food for Your Soul

A Vision

The glory of the Lord descended upon me
and I was transcended from darkness into the marvellous light.
The beauty of the Lord surrounds me and joy fills my soul.
The earthly trappings were shredded from me
as I was transcended towards my God.
My eyes could not believe what I saw;
my mouth could not be contained
as I began to praise the Lord with all my heart.
I was humbled and brought to my knees,
as I witnessed the power of my creator; the Almighty God.
He took hold of my physical shell
and saturated my spirit.
In that moment I felt the awesome presence of the Lord
whom I had always called upon.
My spirit fully yielded in obedience to the Lord
for now I realize that without you Lord I am nothing,
so I thank you for your blessings, your protection,
your love and your presence in my life.
Amen.

TO GOD THE GLORY

… Food for Your Soul

Hope in the Lord

The Messiah came to save the world.
He came to deliver all those who are held captive to sin
saving them from destruction and to offer them eternal life.
Hold fast to the Lord's promise my brethren.
His promise is sure and true.
Deliverance is at hand and the time is short.
Make haste my brethren, get your house in order
so that when the Messiah returns
he will find everything to his satisfaction.
Clear out clutter and discord from your lives,
for the things that are not useful and have no benefit to you
only impedes you and becomes weighty!
Pray, fast and praise to the Lord continually
and you will find that joy, hope, faith, and charity
will fill your house daily.
So make haste my brethren, get your house in order,
for the time is short.
Amen

Food for Your Soul

Change

Seek the Lord with all your heart

and he will uplift you in all your ways.

Desire to love the Lord with all thy heart

and he shall grace you with his presence in abundant.

For he will do good things for man,

but man's heart cannot be corrupted or evil.

His heart and mind must be clean and pure

in order to exercise the will to follow the Lord

and to perform good deeds.

Lord give me the ability to always hear your word

and to draw sustenance from your word.

For just as the body needs food for physical strength,

my spirit needs to be fed with the spiritual food of your word.

I will meditate upon your word to feed my soul,

so that my spirit may flourish in truth and righteousness.

Let my countenance be changed

and let the grace of the Lord be upon me forever more.

Amen.

Food for Your Soul

Cup of Salvation

Lord if I am worthy,
let me drink from the cup of thy salvation and of life,
do not recede it away from your servant
for my soul longs to be quenched of thirst.
My soul needs an anointing from you Lord,
and a pouring out of your blessing upon my life.
Deliver me from this life of woe and tribulation,
and seat me around your table so that I can be fed.
My heart cries out to you Lord, for your saving grace.
For I am in a wilderness, lost and confused, staggering through.
Stretch out your hand to me Lord
and I will be delivered from the storms of life!
O Lord my God, hear my voice as I cry out to you!
Distress surrounds me and perils lay either side of me
but my trust is in Jehovah, the Almighty Lord God of Israel,
whose power is infinite and able to save all who call upon his name.
I shall always declare your faithfulness,
and my lips shall not refrain from sing your praise all day long.

Food for Your Soul

So make haste, make haste and deliver me this day my God.

Amen.

TO GOD BE THE GLORY

Food for Your Soul

I Trust in Thee Lord

Lord as I lay upon my bed of sickness,
my eyes look towards your glory.
The whisper of your name comforts my soul.
My body is racked with pain and my bones ache from fatigue,
I am so fragile!
My endurance is low, as my strength fails me.
The length of my days are only known to you.
The hour, the day, the week, the month, has not been revealed to me.
My strength comes from your salvation
and everlasting promise of eternal life.
So Lord I pray lift me up now,
so that I am able to praise you, adore you, worship you,
whilst I still have breath within my body.
Let my spirit dwell at ease,
for the journey to this place has been long.
Many are the dangers I have surpassed
because the Lord has been by my side.
How then shall I repay this act of mercy?
I shall repay with gratitude,

Food for Your Soul

and tell of the Lord's good mercy towards me in great congregations

and my tongue shall never cease to tell

of the Lord's great love he extended towards me.

For the Lord has shown me great love and compassion.

Therefore I shall be loving and compassionate

to my brother, to my sister, to my neighbour.

The values of the Lord shall be visible within me

and I shall be made new by his hands.

Amen.

TO GOD BE THE GLORY

Food for Your Soul

Strength and Protection

My lips cannot tell of things I know not.
My eyes cannot see what is not revealed to me.
My heart can only express emotions that come from experiences.
Within this universe I am small,
but within God's kingdom I am mighty
because of the love of the Lord towards me.
No army upon this earth can conquer me,
because I am a soldier for the Lord and a warrior for God.
My waist is girded with the truth
and my heart is protected by the breastplate of righteousness.
I am protected by His glory, as I put on the helmet of salvation.
I am protected by His glory,
as I hold the sword of the spirit in my right hand.
I am protected by his glory,
as I hold the shield of faith in my left hand.
I am protected by his glory,
as I march on with the sandals of readiness
to proclaim the gospel of peace.
My enemies have no power over me.

Food for Your Soul

They cannot hold or bind me,
because the victory and the Glory belong to the Lord.

Amen.

TO GOD BE THE GLORY

Food for Your Soul

A Child of the Light

I am a child of the light, created new by the Lord's salvation.
The Lord has poured out his blessings upon me,
creating a new heart, mind, body and spirit within me.
I am truly blessed.
A gift so great He has given me.
I am so grateful for his mercy and his tenderness.
The love of the Lord is evident in my life,
my countenance has been changed
and the Lord has strengthened me.
I am continually pulled towards the beauty of the Lord,
for I have seen the wonderful works of his hands.
My eyes shall remain open and focused upon the Lord
for direction and guidance.
The wisdom and judgement of the Lord is flawless,
and he is his perfect in all ways.
It is not given for me to question His timing
for it is absolutely perfect.
For it is not man's time, but God's time
and nothing shall happen before the time.

Food for Your Soul

Therefore I shall wait on the Lord for his guidance, protection, and my soul shall dwell at peace for I have put my trust in the Lord.

Amen.

TO GOD BE THE GLORY

Food for Your Soul

A Vision of Clarity

The Lord has given me a vision of clarity.
A road was shown to me and a cup I must drink from.
In my vision the road was the path he prepared for me.
I saw perils and dangers either side of the road,
but I was guided on the path by the Lord,
therefore I shall not fear,
for angels were standing by to aid me along the way.
The cup I saw was the cup of salvation I must drink from
to renew my spirit and to rescue my soul from destruction,
and to make me new.
I gladly accepted and drank from the cup offered to me.
Lord, once again, thank you for the honour and the privilege
to worship you with a new heart and a new spirit.
Lord you are so gracious, so merciful and kind to me,
I shall forever praise your holy name.
Hallelujah, Hallelujah

Amen and Amen

Food for Your Soul

A Body Cleansed, a Soul Uplifted

Purify my heart Lord, cleanse my soul.
Let no lie come from my lips.
Cleanse me of all impurities,
so that I may stand in your presence.
Let me refrain from sin and iniquity;
sanctify me Lord for your purpose.
Guide me Lord with your loving hands
and have mercy upon me.
I shall serve you with all my heart,
for my hope is in you; for the perils of this world are great,
so Lord I ask for wisdom and understanding to acquire your ways.
The blessing of a righteous man can always be seen, nothing is hidden.
The fruits of his labour are good
and his strides are strong as he walks through life.
Lord cause me to be a blessing upon this land
as I keep my covenant with you,
my hope and desire is to see the kingdom of heaven
and dwell there for my eternal rest.

Food for Your Soul

My soul shall surely be satisfied
and enjoy the peace of your presence.

Amen and Amen.
TO GOD BE THE GLORY

Food for Your Soul

The Glory of God

I declare the glory of God
and the fullness of his blessings upon my life.
There is rejoicing in heaven when a lost soul is saved,
like the return of the sheep that strayed away
from the flock, Heaven erupts into jubilation.
Great and mighty God protect us from the dangers
and destruction that lurk in secret places.
Protect us from those who come to us as friends
yet in their hearts they harbour malice, envy, hatred
and jealousy, towards their brother or sister.
Let us not be inveigled away from your flock,
for your pastures are green and fruitful.
Outside your love lies a barren land, cold and dry,
no water or pastures can be found there.
It is a place where I would not want a living soul to dwell,
a place full of torment and woe for the soul
cannot flourish or dwell in such a land.
So I thank you Lord for your lush green pastures,

Food for Your Soul

where I am fed and where my spirit flourishes'.

Amen

TO GOD BE THE GLORY

Food for Your Soul

Trust in the Lord

In thee do I put my trust for the Lord is faithful!
In thee Lord do I put my confidence,
for my God is trustworthy and his promises are ever sure!
In thee Lord do I put my hope for you are perfect, flawless
and impeccable! in all your ways.
Lord I ask for protection, day and night,
for he that keeps Israel shall surely protect me.
The burden of sin has been lifted from my shoulders
and the Lord has refreshed my spirit with hope, faith and love.
God is truly great and worthy to be praised.
Thank you Lord for your loving kindness
and tender mercies that you extend to me.
I shall continually praise the Lord God of Israel,
The Alpha and Omega.

Amen and Amen.
TO GOD BE THE GLORY

Food for Your Soul

The Ultimate Treasure

My heart grieves and I am at a loss
to understand how man can be so indignant of God's handy work
and of the marvellous miracles that he performs.
The view of man is sometimes narrow and short sighted.
He fails to see the bigger picture of the plans God has for him.
His concerns are usually of earthly material things
because his vision has no clarity.
His spiritual eyes are closed because of his greed
for earthly possessions.
Man needs to seek the spiritual treasure stored up in heaven,
first he needs to repent of his sins
and invite Jesus to come into his heart.
He needs to let go of the greed
of holding onto earthly material wealth,
then his spiritual eyes will be open
by the Holy Spirit and he will see the reward
that God has for him which is far greater
than any earthly treasures his eyes have ever seen.
Lord I pray for clarity of vision

Food for Your Soul

and for my spiritual eyes to be open,
so that I may look towards heaven,
for I accept Lord Jesus as my saviour
and hold on to his promise of eternal life.
There is no greater gift my heart could desire,
there is no greater treasure I could ever find.
Thank you Lord for my salvation.

Amen and Amen
TO GOD BE THE GLORY

Food for Your Soul

Spirit

Set my spirit free Lord,

for my spirit is not earth bound but heavenly bound.

As I pray uplift my spirit Lord,

so that I may be enlightened and acquire the knowledge

and wisdom that you desire me to have.

Lord please remove all impurities from my spirit

for my spirit belongs to you for eternity.

Let the Holy Spirit dwell with me in perfect harmony.

Amen and Amen.

TO GOD BE THE GLORY

Food for Your Soul

Love Thy Lord God

Love the Lord thy God with all your heart,
with all your soul, with all your might
for He is the creator of all things
in heaven and upon the earth.
The Lord's love for us is incomparable and impeccable!
Let us love the Lord with passion,
vigour, endurance and a pure heart.
Let the love we have for the Lord
be engraved upon our hearts and manifested in our deeds.
For God sees all things and cannot abide falsehood.
The ways of man are known to the Lord,
what we hide form man we cannot hide from God.
For God sees not the flesh!
He sees the heart, the spirit, the soul
and every intent is revealed to him
without our conscious knowledge.
O Lord give me the strength to walk upon this divine path.
The ability to remain steadfast and faithful,
for I know your promise is true

Food for Your Soul

and that you will be with me every step of the way.
O Lord you are truly worthy to be worshiped
because your love is beyond measure.
You have not given me portions
but you have poured your love upon me
in kindness, mercy and blessings.
I thank you Lord with a grateful heart
for I shall always praise you all the days of my life.

Amen.

TO GOD BE THE GLORY

Food for Your Soul

Reflections

Lord you have known me from the beginning of my life.
You know my thoughts, my hopes, my dreams,
without me uttering a word.
As I look back at my life I realise the years have flown by.
My faith in you continues to grow greater each day,
as I gain knowledge and understanding in these latter years.
I shall be useful with the years I have ahead of me,
for I have seen the marvellous creations of your hands
and know that my times are ordained by you.
I shall be selfless in my thoughts and actions towards my brethren,
for the love and mercy which you have shown me in my life
has taught me a great lesson and I shall extend this wonderful love
to my brothers and sisters.

Amen.

TO GOD BE THE GLORY

Food for Your Soul

Meditate Upon the Lord

I shall meditate upon the Lord day and night
for he has rescued my soul from those who seek to destroy me.
From situations that were too difficult for me to manage.
For without cause they took it upon themselves to despise me
and devise ways in which to hurt me.
O Lord let their plans come to nought.
Let them who plan to hurt me be ashamed and confounded.
I shall always put my trust in the God of Israel, because He is just!
My reward is in your vindication
for I know you are righteous and cannot abide deceit.
Lord as I call upon you, deliver me from my enemies
and lift me to a safe abode.
For I shall always glorify your name and sing your praises
for you are the God of my salvation, my deliverer, my saviour!

Amen and amen.
TO GOD BE THE GLORY

Food for Your Soul

The Favour of God

The Lord favours me; He has delivered me from situations
which I could not manage.
The Lord knows my heart and hears my prayers.
The Lord has blessed me amongst many people,
"thank you Lord for your love."
I shall not fail for the Lord is with me!
Who can stand against me?
The Lord protects me from those who seek to hurt me.
My soul and my heart belong to the Lord.
I shall love the Lord
for he has extended goodness towards me
and has saved me from many dangers.
Lord you are truly worthy to be praised!
When I enter in your presence I freely give you the fruit of my lips
because I know where you have taken me from.
I serve you gladly and meditate upon your word
and thank you for the presence of the Holy Spirit in my life.
I shall serve you all my days of my life
and sing praises onto you Lord!

Food for Your Soul

The Lord Protects Me

When men plot to hurt me, the Lord protects me.
He sends his angels to rescue me
with mighty hands they lift me to higher ground.
No harm can befall me when the Lord is with me.
The Lord has given me a new heart filed with faith and strength.
Joy fills my heart to know!
How merciful and kind the Lord has been to me
for when I was in a desolate place weak and faint hearted,
He sent his angels to comfort me and to uphold me.
The Lord has strengthened my spirit
and wiped away my tears of sorrow.
He so is wonderful and worthy to be praised.
Blessed be the Lord God of Israel, the true and living God.

Amen

TO GOD BE THE GLORY

Food for Your Soul

The Path

O Lord I pray, remove the shadows from my life
and saturate me with your radiant light.
Let doubt remain where it is out of sight!
Let faith be my guide and joy be my strength
now that you have come into my life to stay.
For you O Lord have given me purpose and destiny.
Let me not slip, let me not slide along the way.
Let me not stumble but walk with you I pray.
Guided by your loving hands all the way!

Amen

TO GOD BE THE GLORY

Food for Your Soul

A Righteous Path

The path laid for me is clear to see.
O Lord let me not waver, let me not stagger,
let me not stumble but let me be strong.
Let me walk upon the path that you have laid for me
for I have put my trust in thee,
because you promised that once I followed the path you laid for me
you will never leave me nor forsake me.
I need you Lord, day and night,
to guide and protect me on the path
for the path you have laid for me is righteous,
it leads straight to you.
In your loving arms I shall stay,
for Lord you are with me every step of the way.
I thank you Lord, I shall praise your name
for you are my everlasting God.

Amen

Food for Your Soul

The Lord Is Perfect

The Lord is perfect in all his ways.
Peace, love and harmony he gives to us.
Strife, turmoil and turbulence are taken away from our lives
when we come to the Lord.
For in all things God is wise,
a miracle worker, a protector and a guide.
Let us channel our energy into worshiping the Lord
with our heart and our mind
for we shall see the fullness of our God in due time.
A man is judged by the fruits he bears
and the bountiful harvest he produces.
The farmer attends to the plants, adding fertilisers to the soil,
turning the soil and removing the weeds
that will strangle the plants,
so too the Lord protects us and nurtures us as we grow.
The Lord removes all obstacles from our lives,
shielding us from the perils and dangers
Which contains the eternal nutrient so that we will grow

Food for Your Soul

and thrive to our full potential, stepping into his perfect will.

For he will supply's all the provisions.

Lord thank you for your mercy, your love, your guidance,

your protection each and every day throughout our lives.

Amen

TO GOD BE THE GLORY

Food for Your Soul

Confidence in the Lord...1

Let my head be anointed and lifted above my enemies
who came to attack me without a cause.
The Lord is with me
for I have put my trust in the 'Holy One' who protects Israel.
The Lord has seen my heart and knows my desires.
The Lord has taken me on a remarkable journey
so I thank Him with a grateful heart.
He has made my foundations unshakable.
Let me please the Lord in all I do
and let no deceitful words proceed from my mouth,
for the Lord is the keeper of my heart and soul.
My spirit shall dwell at peace,
for I shall not be concerned about the actions of man
whose time is fleeting!
Lord I praise you and I place myself in the palm of your hands.
Let peace and harmony be my song
as I worship you with a joyful heart.

Hallelujah, Hallelujah

Food for Your Soul

Perfect Love

I will construct my life in a positive manner;
I shall be mindful of situations around me, diligent and observant.
I have received wisdom and knowledge in abundance.
The timing of all things is given by the Lord.
The life span of man has become shorter because of sin and
disobedience, but God has been so gracious and merciful towards
man and given us redemption from our Sins
and a hope of eternal life through our Lord Jesus Christ.
God has always loved us, the children whom he created,
it is sin which has separated us from God,
but he loved us so much, he sent his only begotten son Jesus Christ,
who came, and died for us and was resurrected from death.
Jesus stood in the gap for us so let us stand in the gap for each other if
there be a need. The action of our Lord Jesus was the ultimate
presentation of pure and perfect love.
His love endures forever, his path is righteous and his timing perfect.
Let us worship and adore our Lord Jesus, a gift from God our father
and celebrate his life and the sacrifice he made for mankind.
Hallelujah, Hallelujah

Food for Your Soul

A Prayer of Thanks Giving

O Lord my God you are worthy to be praised.

Thank you for your blessings

and the pouring out of your anointing upon me thy servant.

Thank you for healing my broken body

and soothing my troubled spirit.

Thank you for making me whole once again!

As I lift up my hands in praise and worship,

accept my soul as my offering

for I know without a doubt I am precious to you.

The Lord shall keep me safe,

not even the soles of my feet shall be bruised

as I walk upon the path the Lord has laid for me,

for his angels encamp about me.

I shall call upon the Lord day and night

meditating upon his words,

which are a source of comfort and strength to my soul.

I shall be at peace because the Lord holds me in the palm of his hand.

Food for Your Soul

Is love is everlasting and his mercy endures forever.

Hallelujah Hallelujah

Amen

TO GOD BE THE GLORY

Food for Your Soul

Spared From Death

The Lord is my sweet blessed saviour .

I was brought so low

but he lifted me up from the chains of death

and restored my soul to the fullness.

For he has blessed me and spared me from this fate.

I am saved through his grace and mercy,

for the purpose of a higher calling.

I looked and saw how merciful and kind

the Lord had always been toward me.

Great is my God and marvellous are his handiworks.

The nature of things to be shall not always remain a mystery

but shall be revealed in the fullness of time,

through obedience to the Holy Spirit.

For the lord is so precious,

His saving grace, love and mercy

has redeemed me from the perils of the world.

I thank the Lord with a truly grateful heart

Food for Your Soul

and shall continually praise and worship him.

Hallelujah Hallelujah

Amen

TO GOD BE THE GLORY

Food for Your Soul

Faith

Faith is the substance of things hoped for.

It is wrapped up with hope and trust, for by faith we shall obtain.

If we have no faith or little faith we shall not obtain the goals we desire.

If we have great faith then all things are possible.

It is faith alone which shall carry us to heavenly glory.

Faith is the fundamental base of my trust in the Lord.

It is through faith that I shall flourish

and gain knowledge and understanding of God,

a wisdom which is priceless.

Through faith I seek the Lord

and receive all the blessings he has for me.

Glory be to God for all his tender mercies

and unfailing love towards me.

The Lord has been mindful of me,

seen all my afflictions and delivered me out of my calamities.

Amen

TO GOD BE THE GLORY

Food for Your Soul

A Declaration of Love

The Lord has shown great love towards me

and has declared me to be his own.

Blessed be the Lord for he is mighty,

true and merciful towards those who put their trust in him.

He is a faithful God who requires obedience

and faith from us in return.

This payment is pitiful when I consider the rewards of the Lord.

The Lord has placed a wall around me,

an invincible fortress which cannot be penetrated

either physically of spiritually.

For I have made the Lord my trust, my God, My redeemer.

The heavenly host of angels keep watch over me day and night.

No harm shall come near me, either from men or evil devices

because I have put my trust in the Lord

and there is nothing too great for him to do for me.

Blessed be my God the Almighty Jehovah;

The Alpha and the Omega.

Hallelujah,Hallelujah

Food for Your Soul

Strength

A strong man will say "I have great strength"

and will visibly perform feats of strength to impress his fellow men.

But if he does not have God in his life he has nothing,

he is like a shadow upon the landscape

which passes as the sun goes down.

"My strength comes from the Lord."

Blessed be the Lord for every breath I take,

for He makes all things possible!

I am guided by the hands of the Lord!

Who has been merciful and kind to me.

My mouth shall continually praise His works

and lift up His holy name among the multitudes

and great congregations.

Blessed be my God for his great love toward me,

for he is worthy to be praised.

I thank you Lord for your loving kindness and mercy.

I am not a shadow on the landscape but precious am I in your sight!

Amen

Food for Your Soul

The Pure Heart

The desires of the heart are often hidden.

The heart can corrupt the mind and in turn the spirit.

To desire a pure heart is to desire a pure mind and spirit.

The heart is the centre of our emotions

and intangible feelings which are put into thoughts.

Our goal then must always be to desire a" *PURE HEART*"

from which goodness will flow.

Happiness, peace and love will be the products of such a heart.

This can only be achieved by redemption from sin

and commitment to our Lord Jesus Christ.

If I change this physical walk from sin,

then I shall no longer walk in the physical, I walk in the spirit".

Each step I take will be lighter with Christ by my side.

Hallelujah hallelujah

Amen

TO GOD BE THE GLORY

Food for Your Soul

Seek the Lord

Seek the Lord with all thy heart, with thy entire mind,

with all thy might.

Spend time praying to the Lord in solitary places, in thy dwelling.

Make this time holy and devoted.

Through prayer your relationship with the Lord will grow

and flourish beyond all that you could imagine.

For you shall see the rewards of prayers

through the wondrous works His hands shall perform.

Set your heart and mind to meditate upon the Lord,

place him first in your life

for he is the one who gives you wise counselling

when you face problems that seems impossible for you to solve.

For the Lord is the great teacher of knowledge and wisdom.

When grief and sadness fills our heart and life seems unbearable,

go to the Lord for he shall comfort you,

ease the pain and give you perfect peace.

Ask the Lord to banish affliction from your body

Food for Your Soul

and to make you whole again.

For if you pray with faith and vigour,

your request shall be given to you.

So seek the Lord diligently with faith

and spend time with him through prayer,

then all things shall be given to you.

Amen

TO GOD BE THE GLORY

Food for Your Soul

Redeemed

Oh Lord my God you have plucked me from the pit of death

and placed my feet upon solid ground.

You O Lord have made my foundation unshakable,

my trust shall always be in you.

I thank you Lord with a grateful heart.

I shall meditate upon your wonderful works,

the miracles you have preformed

the blessings you have bestowed upon me.

"O Lord your love is beyond compare,

your compassion can not be measured

and you are awesome in all your ways."

Let me be guided by your hands throughout my life

and may you always be near me!

Amen

TO GOD BE THE GLORY

Food for Your Soul

The Word of God

The word of God feeds my spirit and nourishes my soul.

I am sustained and rejuvenated by it.

The manifestations of his word is evident in my life

as it stirs up the LORD to bless me.

My spirit is uplifted whilst I praise him

he is the living bread to my soul.

When I receive the word and plant it in my heart,

it flourishes into gentleness, kindness faithfulness,

goodness, love, joy, and peace, long-suffering and self control,

bearing the fruit of the spirit.

Giving me the character of God.

The word of God is my tool for transformation;

sharper than a two edge sword,

for it shall cut to pieces every deceitful unjust, evil plan of the enemy.

Nothing shall prevail against me,

for I am more than a conquer through Christ Jesus.

Praise and worship is my channel of thanksgiving

Food for Your Soul

and my key to access the presence of the Lord

for I was made to give him the honour the glory and the praise.

So I shall exercise this inherit right at every opportunity

with delight and joy.

I shall praise the Lord, for I know that I am privileged

through grace to boldly enter in His presence.

Amen

TO GOD BE THE GLORY

Food for Your Soul

Gentle Hands

He spoke to me in the stillness of the night

when darkness fell around me.

His voice comforted my soul.

He guided me gently with his loving hands,

His voice reassured me as he repositioned me.

He led me to a place of contentment which my heart had longed for.

I knew that he heard all my supplications and answered all my prayers, for I was the one who had been lost.

Amen

TO GOD BE THE GLORY

Food for Your Soul

The Soft Voice

Harden not your heart as I speak to your soul,

in the stillness of the night!

O Lord I shall adhere to your commands

for your faithfulness is beyond measure, your mercy is endless.

My soul yearns for a righteous life

to live according to your laws to obey you at all times.

I seek strength to deny the things my eyes desire

but my heart dose not seeks.

A strength that no man could give me,

only my sweet saviour could supply.

So in all things I ask

LORD please guide me and protect me along the way.

For my flesh will see corruption

but my spirit shall find eternal rest in the presence

of my heavenly father.

The proud and arrogant man is wasted away

because he is consumed with pride and concerned by appearances.

Food for Your Soul

He gathers material wealth to no avail

while his soul spoils, through lack of spiritual food.

So let me be wise and seek the counsel of the Lord

and place him first in my life.

Amen

TO GOD BE THE GLORY

Food for Your Soul

He Watches over Me

The lord has elevated me and placed my feet on higher ground,

he has comforted me in the night.

He guided me with loving hands through the storms of life.

He has prepared the path for me.

He shall never be far from me,

even if for a moment I dare to think, is he there?

He confirms his Holy presence to me

in subtle ways and marvellous signs.

The presence of the Holy Spirit brings warmth to my heart

and uplifts my soul.

He has blessed me and kept me safe.

I shall continually praise the Lord,

for his mercy is without limit.

His love is endless, his timing impeccable.

Praise the LORD for his good works and for his love.

Amen

Food for Your Soul

How I need you everyday

I need you, need you every step of the way,

A cross to carry no burden to bear.

For you my sweet saviour has paved the way.

How I need you every step of the way.

I need to dwell in your presence and stay,

to make my abode with you today,

a lasting covenant, seal with love and commitment

for I need your hand to guide me all the way.

When perilous times come my way, I need you by my side.

You are the counsellor who equips me

with the solutions to my problems.

You are the teacher who shows me the truth

and orchestrates my path.

You are the comforter who holds me in his hands

and lifts me to higher ground.

O LORD how I need you each and every day.

Amen

Food for Your Soul

Let me be a Blessing

Bless me Lord with your multitude of gifts.

Sanctify me, consecrate me, officiate me,

for I am your ambassador who represents you in the world.

Leave me not nor forsake me,

but elevate me in my times of trials and tribulations

so that your glory and majestic power be revealed to all.

The saints shall give you praise and honour

to see the marvellous works your hands have performed in my life.

An example you shall make of me

and they shall know that these good things came from the Lord,

for you have plans for me and hope for my future.

Lord bless my endeavours and my hands as I give Jehovah the glory and praise.

Amen

Food for Your Soul

An ordered House

Get your house in order for the kingdom of God is at hand,

make ready your house,

for you would not invite a guest into an unclean house.

So take heed my brethren the time is near.

Let no man or woman be found wanting

for on that day there will be no one to hear excuses,

no one to plea or to petition on your behalf.

The Lord will be in your presence on that day

and your works will be held accountable,

so I declare to you,

sons and daughters of man put your house in order

for if your house is not clean then he shall not abide with you.

Clean from inside out,

remove every unwanted thing and clutter from your rooms.

Let the outside of your house reflex the inside.

All shall see it and recognize that this house is clean,

for it will radiate a light like no other

Food for Your Soul

glowing shinning bright day and night.

It shall be a beacon to others

and your Brothers and Sisters shall declare

THIS HOUSE IS CLEAN!!

For we have seen the will of God,

because we have put our trust in him.

To God be the glory for his everlasting love towards mankind

and for the strength that he gives us to perform

the wonderful task he ordain for us.

It is not by our strength that we shall endure

but by the Holy Spirit.

Amen

TO GOD BE THE GLORY

Food for Your Soul

Be Still

"Be still and know that I am God, the Alpha and Omega

You were moulded by my hand."

It was I, who took you out of your mother's womb.

It was I who nourished you as you grew and girded you with strength.

It was I who wiped away your tears during your times of sadness.

It was I who protected you

from unseen dangers trials and tribulations.

It was I who lifted you up many times when you fell.

It was I who comforted you in my arms

when you lost your nearest and dearest.

It was I who healed and quickened you again.

It was I who sustained you on the pathways of life.

It was I who spoke to you in solitary places.

In the stillness of the night

my voice brought comfort to your troubled soul.

I am the one who held you in my arms

as you fell into your final sleep.

Amen.

Food for Your Soul

The works of the Lord

I cried and the LORD wiped away my tears.

My heart was broken with sadness and grief

but the Lord came and comforted me .

He healed my broken heart, I fell and the LORD lifted me up

and placed my feet upon a rock.

He made my foundations strong.

He placed a fortress around me, invincible and invisible to the eye

because I am precious to the Lord.

He has done these marvellous things for me.

When I was faced with worries and pressures of this world,

tears filled my eyes,

I felt two soft hands upon my face

and two fingers from each hand was placed under my lower eye lids.

I felt a gentle rolling rocking motion on my lower eye lids taking place

and I literally felt my tears being pushed back from my eyes.

In that moment I instantly knew

that the Lord had dried my tears and all would be well.

Food for Your Soul

"Lord I thank you with all my heart

for the love I have experienced from you in my life."

I felt when you lifted me up!

I felt when you carried me!

I felt when you wiped my tears and comforted me in your arms.

I felt when you raised me from my sick bed and made me strong again.

Amen

TO GOD BE THE GLORY

Food for Your Soul

Preservation of Life

The Lord has preserved **my** life and strengthen my body.
The Lord sustained me and removed the dark clouds of sickness
which loomed over my head,
He cleared the path and no hindrance came near me.
The power and glory of the Lord are forever,
enduring generations to generations.
The Lord is awesome in all his ways.
His hand gently guides me towards my destiny
and I am covered by his love.
The Lord is righteous, pure and kind,
forever giving and merciful
to those who seek him with sincere hearts.
He is my rock upon whom I lean and rely.
He protects me in the valley as I passed through for he is my Shepherd.
Lord I have felt your loving hands around me,
you were the source of comfort
when sorrow consumed my soul when my heart was broken.

Food for Your Soul

I felt when you wiped away my tears and spoke to me softly.

When I fell during the storms of life,

you carried me and placed my feet on solid ground.

I stood firm because you made my foundations strong,

"O Lord all that I am comes from your love."

Without you I am nothing, with you I have everything.

Thank you Lord for your merciful ways and your loving kindness.

Amen

TO GOD BE THE GLORY

Food for Your Soul

The Righteous Man

The righteous Man shall never perish.
He shall be uplifted in the sight of God.
His head will be anointed
and those who peruse him shall not overtake him
for the lord will scatter them to the wind.
The righteous man is blessed by the Lord.
His righteousness comes from the Lord.
Nothing shall be a mystery in this man
for he shall be like an open book
because he is righteous nothing can be hidden.
His words have substance and truth abounding in them,
as it springs forth from his lips.
The meditation of his heart is acceptable to God.
You will know this man by the sincerity of his words
for they are not empty when he speaks.
Compassion and peace are in his words which comforts the soul.
His deeds are not self centred, there are no ulterior motives

Food for Your Soul

behind his concern for others.

He is not looking for gratitude or self praise

because he is blessed by the Lord.

His righteousness comes from the way he lives his life

because he puts the Lord first in all things.

He is govern by the Spirit of God.

The word of God is hidden in his heart.

He shall be satisfied with long life

and the fat of the land because he is BLESSED.

Amen

TO GOD BE THE GLORY

Food for Your Soul

A Time well Spent

Make some quiet time during the day.

Set this time aside for the Lord.

Use this space of time to speak to the Lord in private.

Share your worries and your cares with the Lord

for a problem which may seem insurmountable to you

will seem as small as a grain of sand to the Lord.

Do not stress or depress yourself with troubles and woes,

hand them over to the Lord to solve.

He has promised to break your yolk and relieve you of your burdens.

Therefore say to the Lord boldly,

"LORD I come to you with these problems

that I am experiencing in my life."

By myself I cannot manage to solve them,

therefore I ask you to find away to solve them for me

because I put my trust and confidence in you!

Amen

TO GOD BE THE GLORY

Food for Your Soul

Standing Naked

We must not stand naked in the presence of the Lord.
We must wrap ourselves in the garment of praise.
This is our covering as we praise and worship the Lord
we are declaring his honour and glory.
Our praise carries a two way blessing;
we are blessing the Lord by the words of praise
which originates from our heart.
During this process our spirit becomes edified
and the Holy Spirit begins to inhabit the praises
and our connection with him becomes tangible.
No one can ever tell you that God is not real,
once you have experienced his presence;
you will never be the same again.
Meeting Jesus brings positive change to people's lives.
My encounter with the Lord as changed my life in so many ways.
Now I am in Christ, in Christ I am a new person.
The former things have passed away and I am now a new creation.

Food for Your Soul

Praise be to my God for all that he has done,

it is marvellous in his sight.

Amen

TO GOD BE THE GLORY

Made New

He made me whole again.

He cleansed my body, renewed my mind, and my spirit.

I was reborn into the glorious light.

The trapping of earthy desires was taken away from me

and I was left to sore to great heights.

To experience spirituality as never before.

I flew like an eagle because the chains of sin were broken.

I have seen great wonders and marvellous things.

I have learnt never to question him,

but always to give thanks and abide with his judgements.

In all things his ways are perfect and his timing impeccable.

The Lord is surely my shepherd and I shall never want,

because he has cleansed me and made me new.

Amen
TO GOD BE THE GLORY

Food for Your Soul

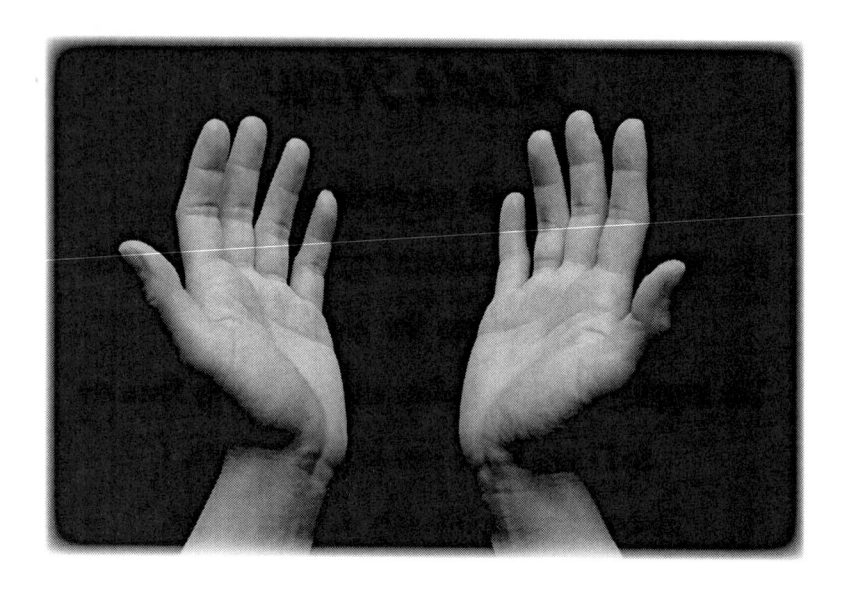

A Prayer Answered

I shall praise the Lord and glorify his holy name

for he is worthy to be praised.

The Lord has given me my heart's desire and answered my prayers.

The Lord has kept me from the path of the destroyer.

He has not allowed my feet to slip.

He has made my house a strong fortress.

The years past are spent and gone;

Food for Your Soul

I now look to the future which is bright and full of hope.

Each day is a blessing and I celebrate it with a grateful heart

for He has blessed me and kept me safe my comfort is in him.

His loving hands re-mould me.

I am now a new vessel for his use.

I shall continually praise the Lord for His loving kindness

and tender mercies towards me.

My heart shall continually seek the Lord.

Amen
TO GOD BE THE GLORY

Food for Your Soul

The Light of the World

Jesus is the light of the world, without him we would be in darkness.

He brings us a light which improves our sight,

giving us knowledge, wisdom and understanding.

Our vision of the world is no longer dull,

compassion, love and a new heart

are the products from an encounter with the Lord.

He took my troubles and cares and throws them away,

so that I could walk upright tall and strong.

I learnt to put my trust in Him

and know that through Christ all things are possible

for He is faithful to the end.

This miracle, this marvel, came about

because I whispered His sweet name

and said Lord forgive me for my sins,

come into my life,

I accept that you lived and died for me and was raised from death.

I accept you as my Lord, my redeemer, my saviour.

Food for Your Soul

A man, who encounters Jesus and opens his heart,

must change as the light of Jesus radiates through him.

This manifestation will be evident in his ways.

He shall enjoy a long life and sickness shall be removed from his midst.

For he shall surely be blessed

because he believes and has put his trust in the Lord.

Amen

TO GOD BE THE GLORY

Food for Your Soul

Words of Comfort

Child hear my voice when I speak to you,

listen attentively to my words, sometimes sent with strangers.

I have spoken words which has touched your heart.

I have been with you when darkness fell.

I have comforted you in the night.

I have travelled with you on lonely roads.

Anger not at things you cannot change,

instead seek to acquire a calm spirit and a vision of clarity,

for anger is blinding and leaves destruction in its paths.

Celebrate life with joy and vitality,

for every moment is a precious gift from God.

Find a quiet time to meditate and pray with faith,

so think carefully about your desires

and make your request known to the Lord.

Faith shall bring you all you desire and seek.

Look forward and not behind,

because what is behind as already gone it is dead,

Food for Your Soul

and cannot be relived or revived.

Instead look to the future and what is ahead.

The pages in front of you are not written as yet.

Weigh your actions, balance them well

for you have been re-moulded

and made new to write the pages ahead of you,

So from this moment live well my child, I shall guild you.

I shall protect you from unseen dangers and calamities.

I shall strengthen you and take your infirmities away from you.

I shall uplift you in your righteous endeavours.

I shall give you shelter from the stormy weather,

you only need to ask, it shall be given to you!

TO GOD BE THE GLORY

Food for Your Soul

A Problem Shared

I faced a problem which seemed like a mountain to climb.

My legs were tired and I was weary,

I looked upwards and asked the Lord to help me,

as I knew I could not manage to solve this problem myself.

I needed His guidance to decide what to do, which path to take.

I needed His protection against evil devises that seek to hurt me.

I needed His comforting hands to wipe away my tears

when I became sad.

I needed His healing powers to take away the pain

and to restore strength to my broken body.

I needed my soul to be renewed.

Oh Lord I could not do without you,

so in all things I shall praise you,

for you are my unseen helper, my deliverer,

my father who comforts me,

my friend who speaks righteously

Food for Your Soul

and offers me knowledge and wisdom.

Without you Lord I would be an empty shell,

blessed be the Lord God of Israel

whose mercy is beautiful and his love enduring.

Amen

TO GOD BE THE GLORY

Food for Your Soul

Love

Love is all that we were meant to be,

an expression of God's love

is where we desire to share with each other.

Love is thinking less of one's self and more about someone else.

Love is everything we were made to be,

it is the open arms of loving parents throughout life.

Love is the birth of a new life entering the world.

Pure and perfect love is our Lord Jesus Christ

who gave his life for us in order that we might have an abundant life.

Amen.

TO GOD BE THE GLORY.

Food for Your Soul

Arms open Wide

God never turns away from us totally,

we are the ones who turn away from Him.

We twist, we turn away from Him,

we wriggle right out of His arms

whilst He stands there arms open wide.

With loving eyes just wanting the best for us.

To know true love is to know the Lord,

for He has pure and perfect love just waiting for you.

Reach out, touch Him, taste and see the Lord is good

and His mercy endures forever,

for He will not utterly cast you aside,

but shall restore you again.

He will not let your affliction over take you ,

your strength fail you, for He will deliver you in your time of need,

for He has sent His Angels on assignment to keep you safe.

So abide in the Lord and He shall abide with you.

Praise the Lord daily and he shall inhabit your praise,

Food for Your Soul

and the blessings will flow for there is none like him.

Amen

TO GOD BE THE GLORY

Food for Your Soul

Material Gain is no Wealth

Learn to recognise a Godly person

as you would a good fruit from a bad fruit.

A Godly person speaks with conviction of the heart.

He does not turn aside is principle for folly or gain in a wimp.

He fears the Lord and worships with reverence.

He stands steadfast in faith

because he or she knows the power of God

and the promise of a righteous life.

There is no earthly gain which compares to such a promise

for men will gather material wealth from now to eternity,

only to leave it behind.

To achieve a righteous life is a far more precious gain.

For such a life is a tribute to God

and an acknowledgement off obedience to God's word.

I shall continually seek the Lord and desire to worship him each day.

I know that the presence of the Lord within my life

is more valuable than anything men may try to offer me.

Food for Your Soul

The Lord is the head of my household and shall be forever more.

Amen.

TO GOD BE THE GLORY

Food for Your Soul

Nothing is Hidden

The ways of men are known to God.
The hearts of men contain secret desires and deeds,
which cannot be seen by the naked eye
or unlocked by human hands but God sees all and knows all.
What is hidden from men is revealed to God without their knowledge.
Nothing under the sun is hidden from the creator,
the Almighty who sustains life and gives life in abundance
without enforced recompense for his services towards mankind.
Let me stand steadfast in the presence of the Lord
who guides my steps, never questioning his judgements
on matters of the heart but let me continually seek his advice.
Elevate me Lord and lift me to higher ground,
so that the perils that surround me will recede.
I shall put my trust in the Lord,
for what is mystery to me as purpose in God's plan for my life.
Strengthen me O Lord and comfort me with your presence,
for I know I shall never be alone with you by my side.

Food for Your Soul

Bless the Lord O my soul forever more.

Amen

TO GOD BE THE GLORY

Food for Your Soul

Pray

Pray earnestly and diligently, He will answer your prayers

because your heart desires it.

So set aside this special time to speak to the Lord

and you will be delighted and surprised

to see the changes that will occur in your life.

Speak from your heart with intensity and boldness.

Focus on the Lord remembering his goodness and mercy.

Know that all things are possible through the Lord

for it is He who girds you with strength

and keeps you through the storms of life.

Draw near to the Lord with the utterance of your lips

and the meditation of your heart.

Apply faith to your prayers, for if you ask you shall receive.

This is your channel of communication with the Lord,

so let it flow and stay connected to the Holy Spirit.

Rest in his presence knowing that when you call upon His name

He will answer you!.

Amen.

Food for Your Soul

We are Vessels

God can make you but He has to break you first.

He breaks you then He re-moulds you and makes you into a new vessel.

He cleans you up because you came to him as a dirty vessel,

He washes you clean and then fills you with goodness,

a new heart, His Holy Spirit with the fruit of the Spirit

and the gifts of the Spirit.

He is the potter and we are the clay.

God has given us a precious gift

more precious than silver or gold,

in the form of the Holy Spirit.

He is absolutely priceless.

To have the presence of the Holy Spirit in my life

is more valuable than anything or anyone.

For He is my comforter, Teacher, Guide my ever present Helper.

Thank you Lord for the precious Holy Spirit.

Amen.

Food for Your Soul

The Holy Spirit

Jesus did not leave me orphan when he ascended to heaven

to be seated at the right hand of God.

He sent the Holy Spirit to be my comforter.

When innumerable troubles surrounded me,

He plucked me from the terrors and held me in his comforting arms.

'Glory to God'

The Holy Spirit is my teacher who teaches me all truth.

He instructs my heart to follow the divine path laid for me,

teaching me right from wrong, good from bad.

Wisdom and understanding is the gift he imparts to me.

'Glory to God'

The Holy Spirit is my guide and counsellor

who speaks to me softly with sound advice

containing compassion, love, peace, and joy.

When I am perplexed and confused,

it is he who unravels the mysteries,

and gives me the solutions to my problems.

Food for Your Soul

'Glory to God'

The Holy Spirit is my helper and my friend,

He is the person who will never leave me or forsake me

when I am in need.

He is a faithful friend, one whom I can depend upon,

He heals my mind and mends my broken bones,

He is my everything.

Amen.

TO GOD BE THE GLORY

Food for Your Soul

Perfect Peace

The perfect peace is a state of balance of the physical body
and the spiritual heart,
achievable only if we relinquish the negative emotional trapping
which anchors us down to negativity.
We are sometimes too concerned with matters
that are irrelevant or trivial, sometimes we even worry
about the things we cannot change
causing us to be in a state of stress and unnecessary anxiety.
If only we would stop and think,
the realisation would enter into our minds
that we cannot solve every problem by ourself
and must therefore hand these problems over to the Lord.
For by faith we shall receive the reward of what we ask for,
so we must never be doubtful or negative
when making a request to the Lord.
We must come boldly and confidently before him,
knowing that the Lord knows what we need before we ask.

Food for Your Soul

We should always be mindful and careful about what we seek
and desire, making sure that our desires and aspirations
are not detrimental to our physical and spiritual wellbeing.
So when we hand over or make known to the Lord our desires,
we must ask him to give us guidance and protection
in all areas of our lives,
to accept the things we cannot change
and to desire only what is good for us.
In doing so we will achieve a state of spiritual contentment
and physical wellbeing; a state of perfect peace.

Amen

TO GOD BE THE GLORY

Words of Encouragement

Food for Your Soul

Words of Encouragement

Purpose

God has a purpose for you and I, our natural mind can direct us from our divine path to a natural path imposed by the mind but when we walk in obedience to God the Holy Spirit supernaturally align us to the divine path for the word of God says obedience is better than sacrifice.

When we sacrifice something we deny ourselves. Our sacrifice must be worthy, it must be of value. If it does not cost us anything then it is not a sacrifice, as we walk in obedience it satisfies God because He does not require sacrifice and burnt offerings.

Jesus has made the ultimate sacrifice for us, He paid a price that no man could ever pay. He gave His life willingly for mankind paying the ransom for our sins. He redeemed us by His precious blood.

Now God requires us to walk in obedience by keeping our bodies as a living sacrifice Holy and acceptable to him. God tells us that this is our reasonable service to him.

Jesus released us from the bondage of sin by giving his life therefore it is reasonable that we keep our bodies sanctified and consecrated to him. When we commit our lives to the Lord and walk in obedience to his word then we become the living sacrifice that God desires.

Amen.

Food for Your Soul

Woman

Woman thou art Beautiful, crafted by skilful hands you are a precious jewel in my crown.

Woman thou art Beautiful, learn to value yourself for silver and gold cannot compare to you, for you are my special treasure.

Woman thou art Beautiful the essence of sensitivity, compassion and nurturing was deposited into your spirit when my hands moulded you.

Woman thou art Beautiful you are the gentle side of me. A giver and receiver, peace was on my mind when I created you. I gave you hands that would dry tears, comfort the wounded spirit, make friendships, feed empty stomachs not to bend a bow or put to war.

Woman thou art Beautiful, these are just a few of the many qualities I have given you. Take a spiritual excavation and release all the possibilities I have deposited in you. For your strength is inwards not outwards, you are certainly not the weaker of the two.

You are stronger more than you realise.

Through the Holy Spirit find yourself.

Words of Encouragement

Love yourself. Value yourself.

Because WOMAN thou art BEAUTIFUL.

Food for Your Soul

The Power of Prayer

Prayer is our divine channel of communication with God and to God. It is this dialogue between us and God during our times of prayers which causes us to meditate upon the goodness of the Lord. Prayer doesn't have to contain elaborate words or eloquent speech.

Simple prayers are the most effective.

When you are in a dark place where you feel trapped where you cannot see a way out where you cannot find the words to express your dilemma, then by just simply turning to God and saying:

'Lord help me'

that is a prayer for He knows your situation, He feels your pain. These few words speak volumes to God because you are saying Lord I cannot solve this problem myself, I put my trust and confidence in your power to deliver me from the situation to change the course of my life,

Lord you are able to do the impossible.

Lord I am weak and without strength, so I need your joy and your peace, which surpass my understanding. A few spoken words can mean so much to God when it comes from a sincere heart and when

Words of Encouragement

faith is applied.

Lord I am weak in my circumstances. I am not able in my strength, only with the Holy Spirit I am able to withstand and stand steadfast to accomplish the purpose and divine destiny that the Lord has for me.

Amen.

TO GOD BE THE GLORY.

Food for Your Soul

The Pathway

Knowing that you are on a pathway
divinely given orchestrated by God's loving hands.
He is the navigator, the creator of all things
in Heaven and Earth nothing is hidden from him.
We are exposed to him because He crafted us.
Temptations are thrown into our path to build our character
and for us to totally put our trust in the Lord.
God has not tempted us, our desires have lead us to the challenge.
The enemy will battle our minds
and try to reason his way through the temptation
but because we have the gift of the Holy Spirit
He will tell us all truth.
Remember Job,
if you have everything the enemy will try to make you lose it.
The enemy comes to steal your dreams and aspiration.
If we give into temptation he kills our walk
and our destiny hangs in jeopardy.

Words of Encouragement

Remember God always has a plan for you to give you a future, a life of pleasure, in him.

Amen

TO GOD BE THE GLORY

Food for Your Soul

Renewing your Spiritual Passion

Spiritual Sluggishness'

Jesus had passion for us, His passion for us led Him to the cross and to victory through His resurrection. Passion is the driving force which propels us to higher heights and deeper depths in Christ. Passion contains Vision, Love, and Determination.

Hebrew 12 v 1-3 states:

"Therefore we also, since we are surrounded by so great a cloud of witnesses, let us lay aside every weight and the sin which so easily ensnares us and let us run with endurance the race that is set before us. Looking unto Jesus the author and finisher of our faith, who for the joy that was set before him endured the cross despising the shame, and has sat down at the right hand of God. For consider Him who endured such hostility from sinners against Himself, lest you become weary and discouraged in your souls."

This text speaks of persistence in passion. Our life in Christ is compared to a race and the writer tries to convince us that we must run the race with endurance if we plan to finish well. We cannot waiver, we must pace ourselves, we must have vision, focus, purpose, stamina, and

Words of Encouragement

tenacity. The text also suggests that we have to set our minds to unlocking passion by using the key of persistence, and then use the key of passion to unlock purpose. We have to get serious about finishing well.

We must be determined and focus on the things of God. We have to watch out for every trap that the enemy will set; laying aside every impediment that would prevent us from finishing well.

Matthew 26 v41 States:

"Watch and pray, lest you enter into temptation .The spirit indeed is willing, but the flesh is weak."

The flesh is constantly warring against the Spirit it desires to satisfies itself. It continually cries out to be fed by carnal acts of the body, whereas the Spirit desires to please God. We are called to worship God in spirit and truth. We are renewed in the spirit of our mind by applying the word of God to our life. A well established prayer life and worship brings us into the presence of the Lord. Being filled with the Holy Spirit is vital to spiritual growth and spiritual balance. Daily devotion

Food for Your Soul

to read and apply the word of God to our life, refreshes our spirit and brings forth much spiritual fruit.

The Spirit filled life gives us power and the ability to be overcomers. The Apostle Paul calls you to put on the whole Armour of God that you may be able to stand against the wiles of the devil. For we do not wrestle against flesh and blood. The Armour is given to us as a new spiritual garment, that we must put on in order to walk the spiritual path. It must never be removed for our warfare is spiritual.

We are called to be on duty at our post 24 hours per day, 7 days per week 52 weeks per year for life.

We must be immovable resolute, defiant in the work of our Lord and saviour Jesus Christ. Our appetite for the things of God must be insatiable, constantly seeking higher heights and deeper depths in Christ.

"Therefore Saints Beware of Spiritual Sluggishness"

This is when a believer becomes weary, spiritually tried and lethargic The person is present in Body but absent in mind. The person is present in church, but their mind is elsewhere. Their mind is at home, at work, on relationships, on finances wondering from issue to issue. It is a state

Words of Encouragement

of dullness to God and a lack of spiritual energy characterised by sluggishness. We become detached from church gatherings or from taking part in ministry or social events within the church, making excuses and reasoning with oneself about staying at home, not fellowshipping, not getting involved. God's solution for this condition can be found in:

Hebrews 10 v 25 the word of God states:

"Not forsaking the assembling of ourselves together, as is the manner of some, but exhorting one another and so much the more as you see the day approaching."

That day being The Awesome Day the Lord will return to us. So saints let us watch out for one another being sensitive to each other's needs encouraging each other, lifting each other up, through positive words and actions and never lose our passion for the Lord.

TO GOD BE THE GLORY

Food for Your Soul

Strength...

Men faint away when trouble surrounds them. All strength leaves and melts away. We are sometimes consumed by our desires. We are sub consciously lured away by them. God does not tempt us but He does observe where we stand in the temptation.

Testing shows our strength and identifies our weakness, our frailty or inability to stand by the very words that we speak and the promises we make to ourselves and to others.

Sometimes a person's weakness can lead to psychological and physical dependency.

What are people hooked up too?

Hooked up to Drugs

Hooked up to Gambling

Hooked up to Stealing

Hooked up to Lies

Hooked up to Strife

Words of Encouragement

Hooked up to Prostituting

Hooked up to Adultery

Hooked up to Fornication

Hooked up to Abusive Relationships

Hooked up to Gangs

All these actives require the submission of a person's will power giving raise to dependency leading to weakness. The enemy uses these weaknesses to keep us in darkness.

Submission to the flesh leads to Spiritual Death.

The carnal mind is sensual and demonic in nature.

The Apostle Paul says, He dies daily to sin, because the same sin we died to yesterday will rise up again today and tomorrow.

The flesh will rise up but by renewing our minds we are transformed, so that the things we use to do we do them no more for a new law now governs us. Jesus says comes as you are, and we come to him all messed up hooked up, violated like a city who's walls have been broken down; but He didn't tell us to remain that way.

Food for Your Soul

He says:

"*BE TRANSFORMED* by the renewing of your mind."

He opens our spiritual eyes to our sinful nature and gives us a new heart for the things of God. The Holy Spirit rebuilds us by teaching us all truths.

This is accomplished through applying the word of God to our daily living. The word is spirit and life. God gives us his peace, which sooths our soul and strengthens our spirit. The peace of God comes upon us, which surpasses our limited understanding. For in my strength I am weak, I can do nothing but through Christ who strengthens me I can do all things. Fear is my enemy; it comes to enslave my mind capturing my thoughts, putting me in bondage to sin.

Fear requires the submission of my spirit but God did not give me a spirit of Fear but of power to overcome, of love to cover a multitude of sin and to endure. A sane mind to praise him so the enemy as to flee. When I think I am strong, I am weak. It's ok to say I can manage, I can cope with whatever comes my way but when deep waters surround me, am I able to reach the shore?

Words of Encouragement

When trouble knocks at my door am I able to stand or when my back is against the wall, will God make away out of nowhere so that I can escape to higher ground?

2 Corinthians 12 v10 states:

"Therefore I take pleasure in infirmities, in reproaches, in needs, in persecutions, in distresses, for Christ's sake. For when I am weak, then I am strong."

When our natural strength fail us, Gods strength is made perfect in us. The core of our Christian life from beginning to the end is lived through faith in Jesus Christ. Our spiritual strength lies in the power of Jesus operating within us as we walk in obedience to Him, He is then able to pour into our vessel His awesome love, for He tells us we are:

"more than conquerors through Christ Jesus."

So I know when I am weak I am strong. I will lean on the Holy Spirit the comforter who will deliver me and restore my strength for another day, for His grace is sufficient for me.

TO GOD BE THE GLORY

Food for Your Soul

The Desire of Hannah's Heart

1st Samuel Chapter 2 v 1-10

Hannah knew the power of prayer. In this prayer she says

"My heart rejoices in the Lord".

God had changed her circumstances that she had endured so many years. She was barren but she didn't ask her husband for a child. Hannah asked the Lord because she knew she needed divine help! God blessed her with her heart's desire, a child because she spoke from her heart when she prayed to the Lord. The Lord took away despair, bitterness and anguish from her heart and replaced it with joy and hope.

v7 –8 Says:

"He brings low and lifts up. He raises the poor from the dust and lifts the beggar from the ash heap, to set them among princes and make them inherit the throne of glory."

Our current circumstances does not determine our future. God can reposition us for greatness, once we walk in obedience to him.

Words of Encouragement

God took away the reproach of barrenness from Hannah and gave her fruitfulness.

Prayer allows us to activate the powers of God to restore, deliver, heal; and allows us into enters into his divine presence.

TO GOD BE THE GLORY

Food for Your Soul

A Mighty Woman of God

Judges Chapter 4

Deborah – meaning Honey Bee

The function of the Honey Bee is to collect and cross pollinate flowers and crops. They produce nectar which is turned into honey. A Bee is an industrial creature, playing a vital role enabling crops to produce a plentiful harvest. The harvest that Deborah brought to her people as a Judge was victory in a war followed by 40 years of peace. Deborah functioned in the capacity of a Prophetess, Judge and Military Advisor, who had supernatural knowledge of warfare.

A wife and Mother, A mighty woman of God! She reigned for 40 years. I believed that she was much loved and highly respected, the only woman in a male dominated time.

Barak the captain of the Army would not go to war unless she came with him, although she told him that the glory and victory would be given to the hands of a woman.

Words of Encouragement

God does not require women to be voiceless in the church, once we are obedient and submissive to His will, God will reveal and establish the purpose which He has for us as women in His Kingdom.

Every woman in the kingdom of Christ as been blessed with gifts from the Lord. God has made a deposit into our spirit for birthing once we accept Jesus as Lord and Saviour and walk in obedience to God's will. It is this deposit, this seed, this gifting that the enemy flights against, hence the scripture

Ephesians chapter 6 v12

"We do not wrestle against flesh and blood, but against principalities..."

TO GOD BE THE GLORY

Food for Your Soul

A Personal Invitation to the Great Supper

Luke Chapter14 -v16-24

Many were invited to the Great Supper and they should have been honoured to attend but instead they came up with all manner of excuses. The Master became angry and sent the servants to go out quickly into the streets and the lanes of the city, the highways and hedges. He told his servants to bring in the poor and the maimed and the lame and the blind, people who needed something from Him, People who are not self sufficient but people who had a real need.

The time will come when the Lord, will get fed up with our excuses and we may find that the door to the supper is closed to us. When we make an excuse to the lord we have taken ourselves out of the will of God we are actually being disobedient, by not submitting and surrendering our will to Him.

Words of Encouragement

We are therefore not being led by the Holy Spirit, because our flesh full nature as risen up, which is an enmity to God. Jesus needs us to be totally committed to him, being a disciple of Christ means total rejection of all our self centred nature for the sake of following, and living for Jesus. If we want to experience and achieve Gods purpose in our lives, we have to make and maintain total commitment to him. The cost is high but the rewards are great!!

TO GOD BE THE GLORY

Food for Your Soul

Wounds

When we accept Jesus as Lord and become a member of his body, we will go through times of testing, within the confines of the brother hood. We are allowed to experience spiritual wounds that the enemy will inflict upon us from time to time. This is a part of the journey.

Our trials and tribulations are minute compared to the magnitude of suffering experienced by our Lord and saviour Jesus Christ upon the cross at Calvary.

Jealousy, envy, malice, hatred, slander and false witnesses came against him.

He experienced all this before he was tortured and nailed to the cross, yet he was silent as a lamb before the slaughter. Before He died He asked Father God to forgive us for what we had done to him. What we did to him He could not hold against us because he loved us so much! The love of Jesus heart covered the multitude of our sins and He gave himself as a willing sacrifice for us which went up to God as a sweet smelling aroma.

The testing times we experience are to perfect changes in our character

Words of Encouragement

and allow us to experience wounding without death. I want to encourage you by telling you that when you are going through difficult times and terrible situations don't be lead away by your emotions, about how you feel regarding your circumstances, instead I recommend that you allow the Holy Spirit to place his loving arms around you and take the instructions He will give as He walks with you through the valley, for the Lord says once you accept him, He will never leave you nor forsake you.

When I think of the goodness of the Lord these are the qualities I find in him;

He is the resurrection and life.

He is the silent listener to our conversations

He is in the mist of two and three as we gather in his name.

He is my redeemer and way maker.

His blood made atonement for my sins.

He reconciled me to God.

He is my king.

He is my provider.

He is my healer.

Food for Your Soul

He is my mediator.

He is hope, He is peace.

He is the High Priest who intercedes for me.

He is my counsellor.

He is everything that I have search for all of my life,

everything I need is in him.

TO GOD BE THE GLORY

Words of Encouragement

The Power of the Tongue

Proverbs 18 v 21

Death and life are in the power of the tongue and those who love it will eat its fruit.

As believers in Jesus Christ we must learn to control our tongue. Knowing when to speak and when to be silent, how to use words that will build, bless, and restore a person . This shows spiritually maturity, whereas spiritually immature people have loose tongues saying any thing that comes into their minds.

When you are about to say something which will set discord, cause contention and hurt, bite your lips refrain from speaking hold your tongue with a bite and bridle. In so doing no offense will proceed, no contention will be caused. No malice will be inflicted; no hurtful negative destructive words will flow out of your mouths.

Subdue that tongue! By allowing the Holy Spirit to harness it. Sometimes people will say very hurtful words to us which literally cut into the very core of our spirit and wound us just as if they took a knife

Food for Your Soul

and stabbed us. These are the words that wound our spirit causing spiritual death.

A wounded spirit is harder to win back than a strong city, speaks of such an effect.

Jeremiah 17 v 9

The heart is deceitful above all things and desperately wicked, who can know it? It seeks and harbours wickedness:

"Out of the abundance of the heart the mouth speaks"

We are condemned by our own words, since there is no condemnation in Christ Jesus! So we need to regulate check, examine ourselves and be transformed by the renewing of our minds applying the word of God to our lives. We can't be just hearers of the word, we have to be doers of the word.

The spirits of the Tongue.

The talebearer - carries news which wasn't theirs to carry usually bad

Words of Encouragement

news. The facts are distorted and does not resemble the original conversation. The essence of the truth is mixed with lies.

The Slander – slaughters without mercy or compassion whose mouth spites out poisonous words of untruth. The aim of this tongue is to assassinate a person's credibility and annihilate their character.

The Gossiping Tongue

This tongue is totally out of control it is loose, it strives to cause division and contention. This tongue is restless and destructive it boast untruths, malice, pride, jealousy, and is judgemental. The power of the tongue sends Angels on assignment.

James 5 v15 – states

"The effective fervent prayer of a righteous man avails much."

But the same power in the tongue sends demons on assignment to carry out the enemy's work. We have to be careful about the words which we speak.

Imagine as you speak into the atmosphere there are Angels snatching the good words to go on assignment for you. If you speak negative words, demons snatch those and go on assignment for the enemy. When praise and worship becomes our lifestyle and the Lord is the focus of our conversations demons cannot stick around!

Therefore we must be sparing with our words. We must guard the words which proceed from our mouths, they must reflect JESUS!
If you are going to say something, think before you speak, ask yourself would Jesus say this? If the answer is no then don't say it.

Likewise with your actions is this what Jesus would do, if the answer is no then don't do it. Jesus is our ultimate example, the original blueprint for how we should live our lives as his disciples.

My final word of encouragement –

The words we use come to weigh us and ultimately judge us!
They must be words which;

Words of Encouragement

Encourage not discourage

Build not tear down,

Restore not destroy,

Heal not wound,

Comfort not contentious,

Wise not foolish,

Peaceful not hurtful,

Enlightened not confusing.

Above all they must be loving not hateful.

We must remember our words have cause and effect!

Let us meditate on these things.

TO GOD BE THE GLORY

Food for Your Soul

How Committed are you ?

Commitment – Sold out, reliable, sacrifice, engaging, selfless, trustworthy, loyal, dependable, working towards the goal of completion.

In order to be committed you have to know the vision. As a Christian I am committed to Christ, I bear His name to be Christ like and to follow his teaching as one of His Disciples. This requires devotion obedience and discipline.

Through the commitment Jesus made to us by dying for us on the cross. He paid the ransom for our sins and redeemed us by His precious blood,so when I am having a difficult time or when someone upsets me or I can't get my own way, it doesn't give me permission to opt out of my commitment to my ministry or to the church, the brethren or to fellowship.

My commitment should never and can never depend on how I am feeling for the vision is far greater than me!

Words of Encouragement

I am a part of the puzzle that makes up the picture. If my commitment depends on how I am feeling, then this will be seen as a battle area for the enemy. If we are swept away by negative emotions and circumstances then, our ministries are robbed, whilst we are not in the position we should be.

It maybe that someone is saved through a song that Sister Denise sings today or someone is encouraged by a word from Mother Livingstone or someone feels welcome by Sister Charlene as they enter the Church and is escorted by her to their seat, or simply someone feels loved and appreciated as you greet them during the service.

A beautiful story, which speaks of commitment is told in the book of Ruth, having lost their husbands and both being widows, wanting to return to her home land, Naomi instructed Ruth her daughter in law to return to her country and her people the Moabites but Ruth loved Naomi and said to her;

    "entreat me not to leave you or to turn back from

Food for Your Soul

following you! For where you go,
I will go and wherever you lodge I will lodge.
Your people shall be my people and your God my God!
Where you die, I die and there will I be buried.
The Lord do so to me and more also if anything but death,
parts you and me!"

Through Ruth's commitment obedience, devotion and love, God turned her life around and lifted her to another level. She met and married a rich man called Boaz and became a part of the linage of Jesus. She had a child named Obed and Obed had Jess and Jess had King David.

Final Word

I encourage you to stay focus and committed to the Lord. Catch the vision of his kingdom by staying in your ministries and let God perform wonders in your life. Commitment involves you making a decision, so remember your attitude determines your altitude.

TO GOD BE THE GLORY

Words of Encouragement

The Power of the Blood and Victory through the Cross

The cross, a Roman symbol which represented death, an instrument used for torture and public humiliation; bringing forth an agonizing death to the recipient.

This symbol of death became a symbol of life through Jesus Christ.

John Chapter 10 verse 10

Jesus said: "the thief does not come except to steal to kill and destroy, I have come that they may have life and that they may have it more abundantly."

The sacrifice of Jesus on the cross gave a new meaning to this symbol bringing forth spiritual fruits for the believer. His sacrifice brought redemption, freedom ,salvation, restoration, reconciliation, love and access to the throne room of God.

Food for Your Soul

To many people in the world, the cross has become a fashion statement, worn as accessory for pleasure. People wear it not knowing or accepting the real message of its value and sacrifice.

Psalm Chapter 40 verse 6-8

Speaks of this sacrifice, it states:

"Sacrifice and offering you did not desire, but a Body you have prepared for me. In burnt offerings and sacrifices for sin you had no pleasure. Then I said, Behold I have come in the volume of the book it is written of me to do your will O God."

The blood of Jesus gives us access and acceptance to God for His sacrifice gives us remission of sin, and sanctifies us.

God sees us through the Blood of Jesus, he sees us righteous, made right with him through the obedience of Jesus.

He sees us complete in Christ, lacking nothing, everything that belongs to Christ belongs to us.

The starting point of faith believes what the Lord says about us.

He says:
                        To come to him

Words of Encouragement

To follow him
To love him
To trust him
To love others as we love ourselves

Jesus gives us the grace to be obedient, through the Holy Spirit, for we can't be obedient in our strength it is achieved through the power of the Holy Spirit, transforming the spirit of the mind.

Colossians Chapter 1 verse 19-22

States, for it pleased the Father that in him all the fullness should dwell, and by Him to reconcile all things to Himself, by Him, whether things on earth or things in heaven, having made peace through the blood of His cross.

And you, who once alienated and enemies in your mind by wicked works, yet now He has reconciled in the body of His flesh through death, to present you holy and blameless, and above reproach in His sight if indeed you continue in the faith, grounded and steadfast, and are not moved away from the hope of the gospel which you heard, which

Food for Your Soul

was preached to every creature under heaven, of which I, Paul, became a minister.

The final Word comes from:

Hebrews Chapter 9 verse 12

"Not with the blood of goats and calves, but with His own blood He entered the Most Holy Place once for all, having obtained eternal redemption."

So we must walk in the promise of eternal life in full assurance, knowing that our body is corruptible but our spirit is eternal.

"To be absent from the body is to be present with the Lord."

TO GOD BE THE GLORY

Words of Encouragement

Your Notes...

Food for Your Soul

Notes

Food for Your Soul

Notes

Food for Your Soul

Notes

Food for Your Soul

Notes

Food for Your Soul

Notes

Food for Your Soul

Notes

Food for Your Soul

Notes

Food for Your Soul

Notes

Lightning Source UK Ltd.
Milton Keynes UK
UKOW03f0746151013

219079UK00005B/65/P